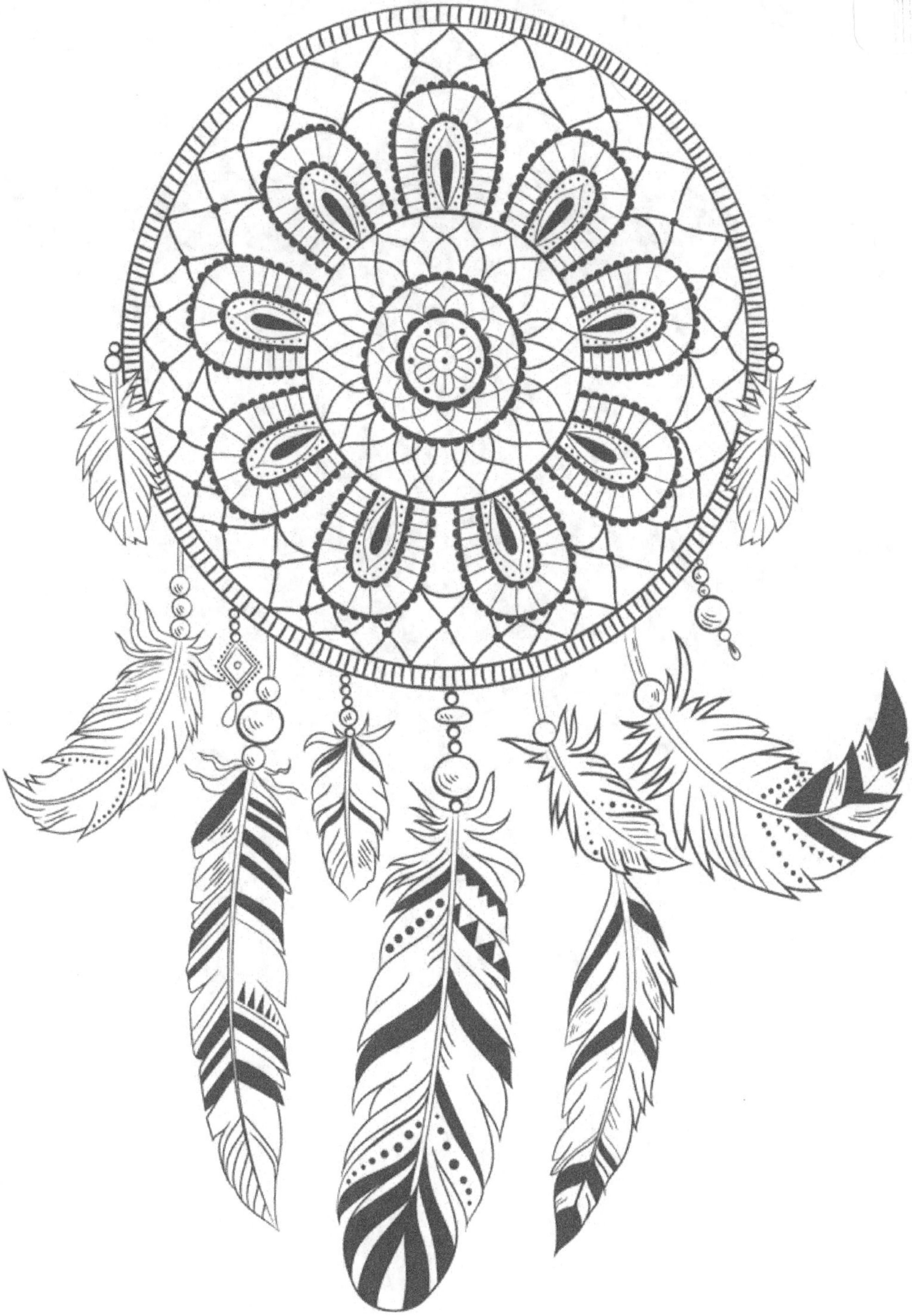

# DREAM CATCHER COLORING BOOK FOR ADULTS

## Copyright © 2020 Katrin Stark

# This Book Belongs To:

_____

_____

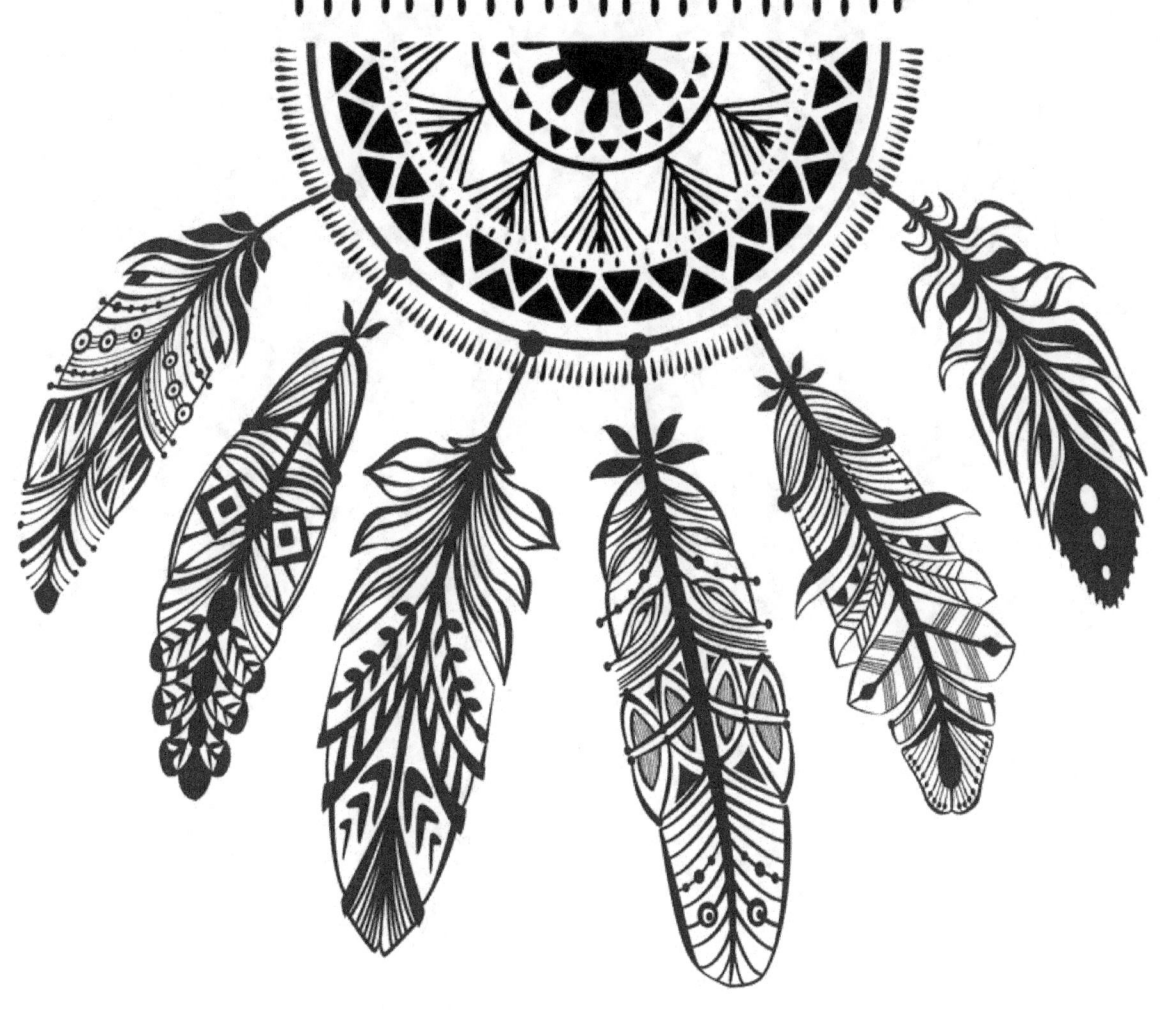

# COLOR TEST PAGE

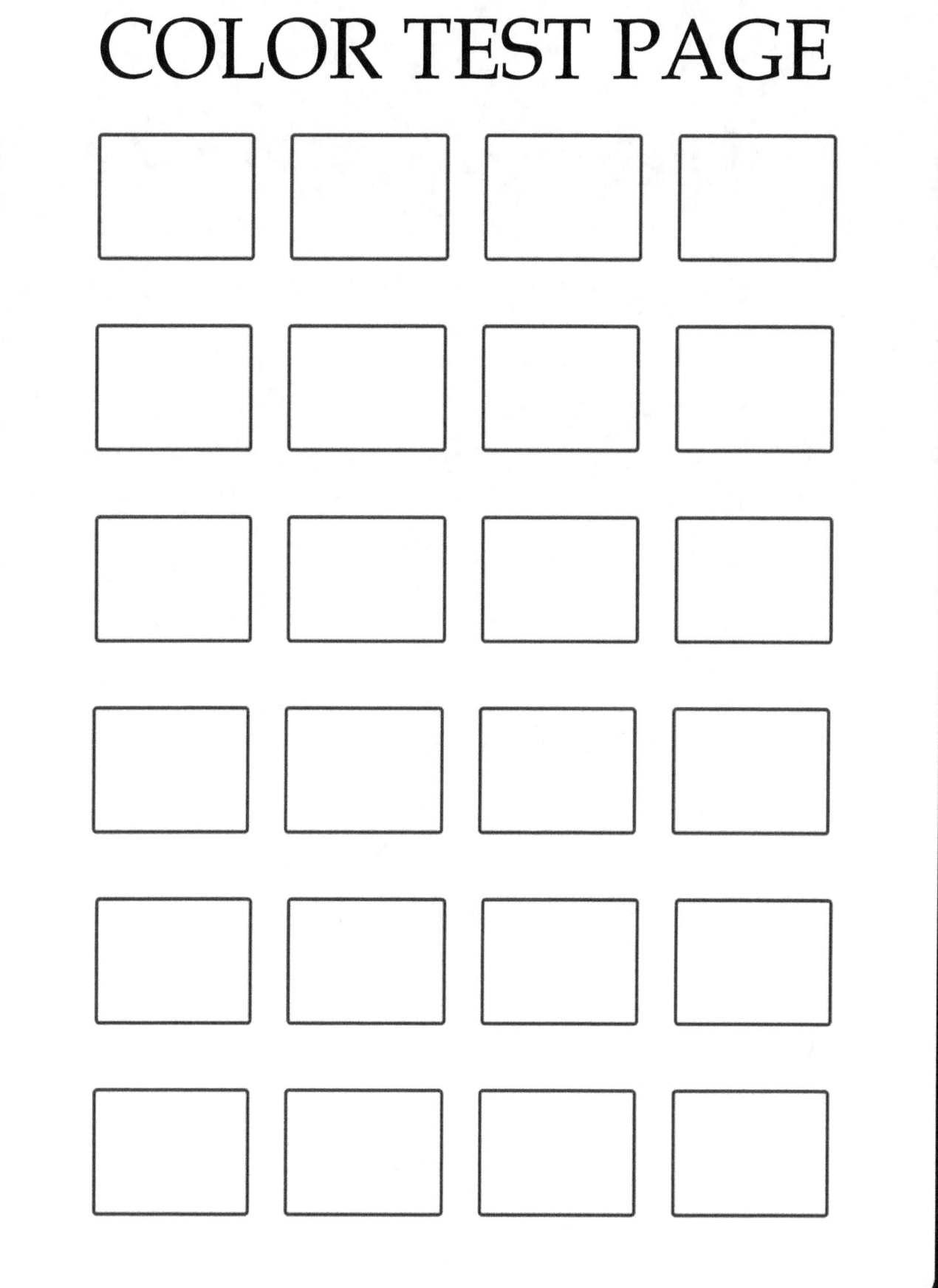

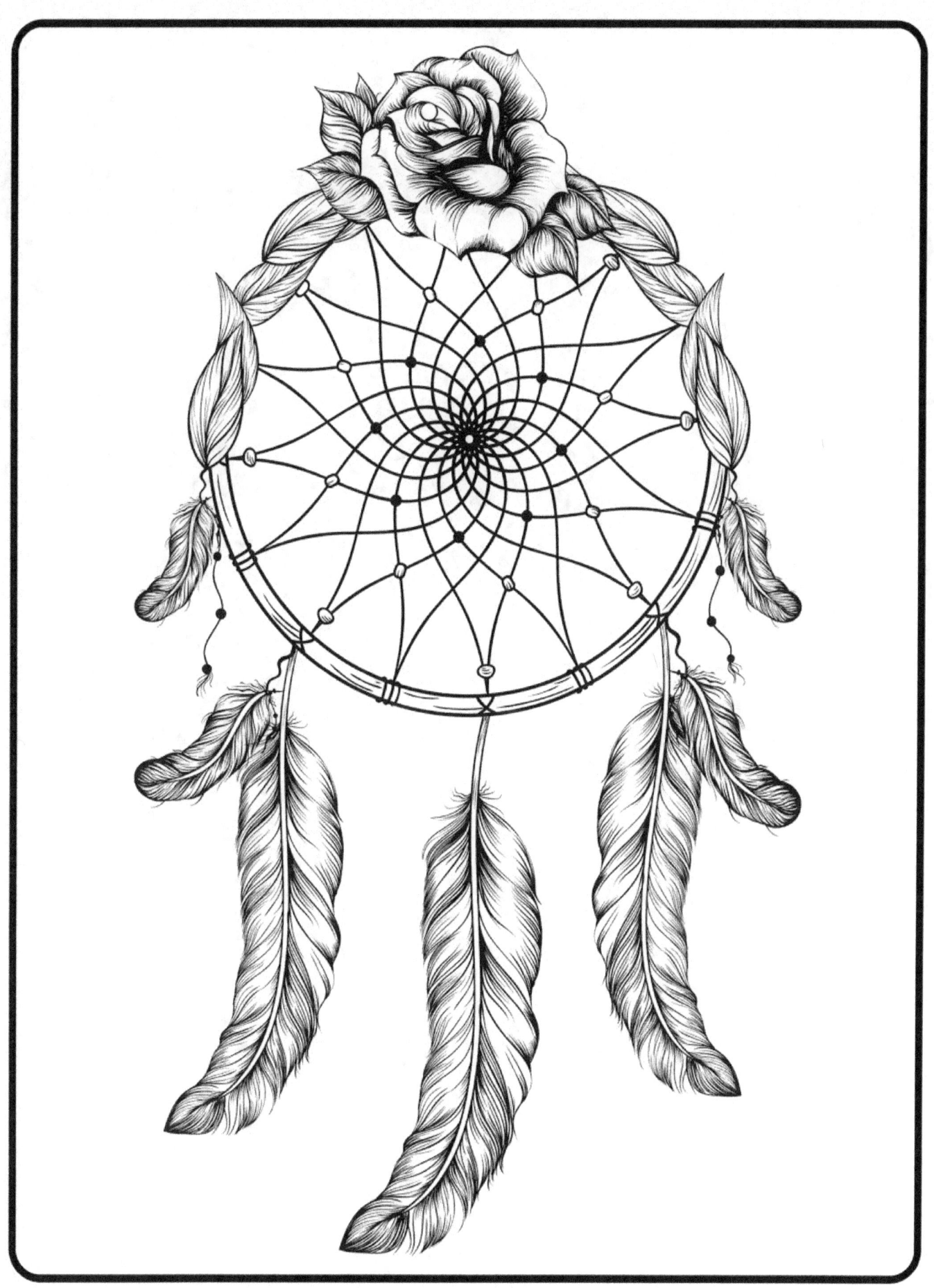

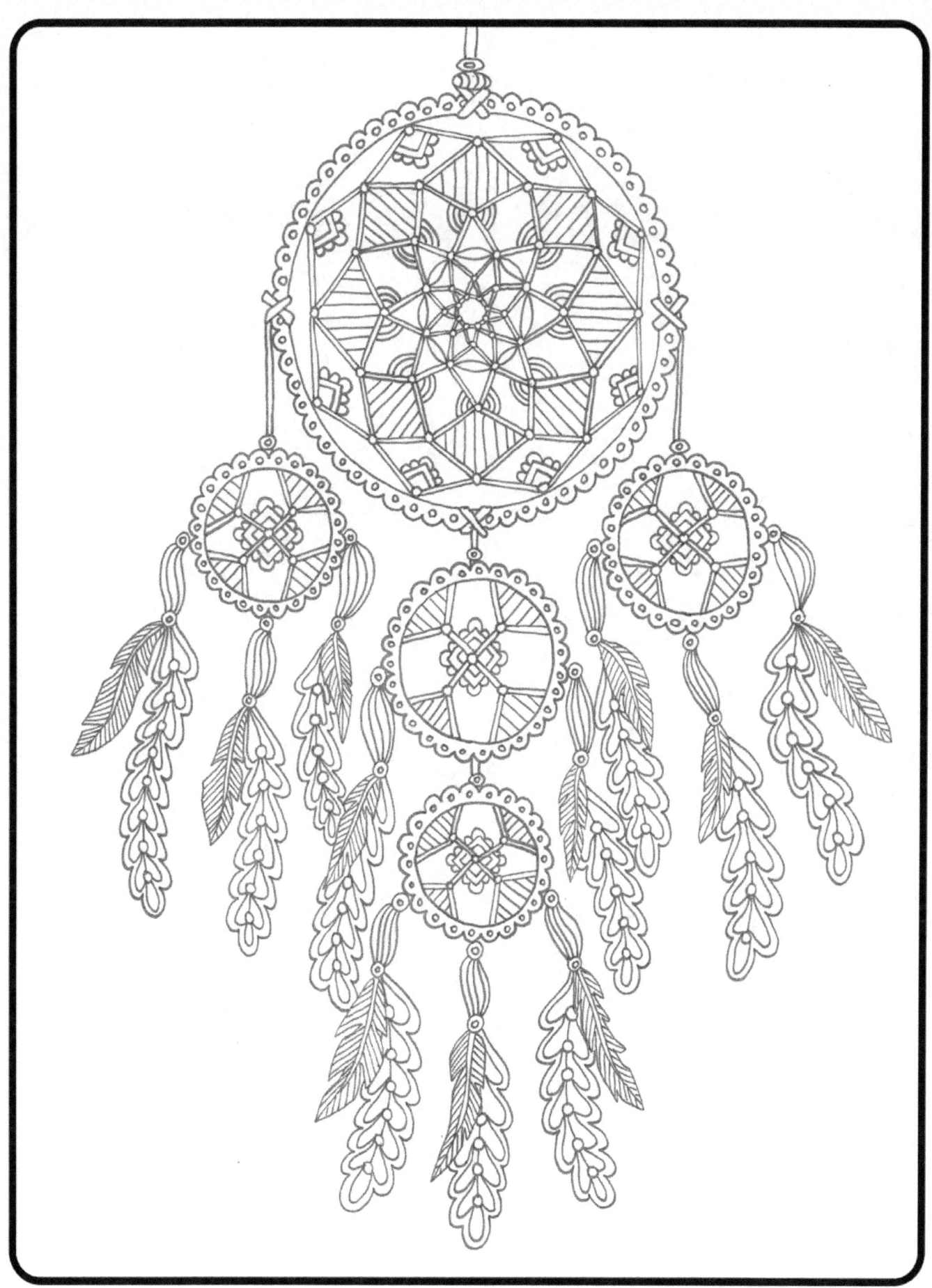

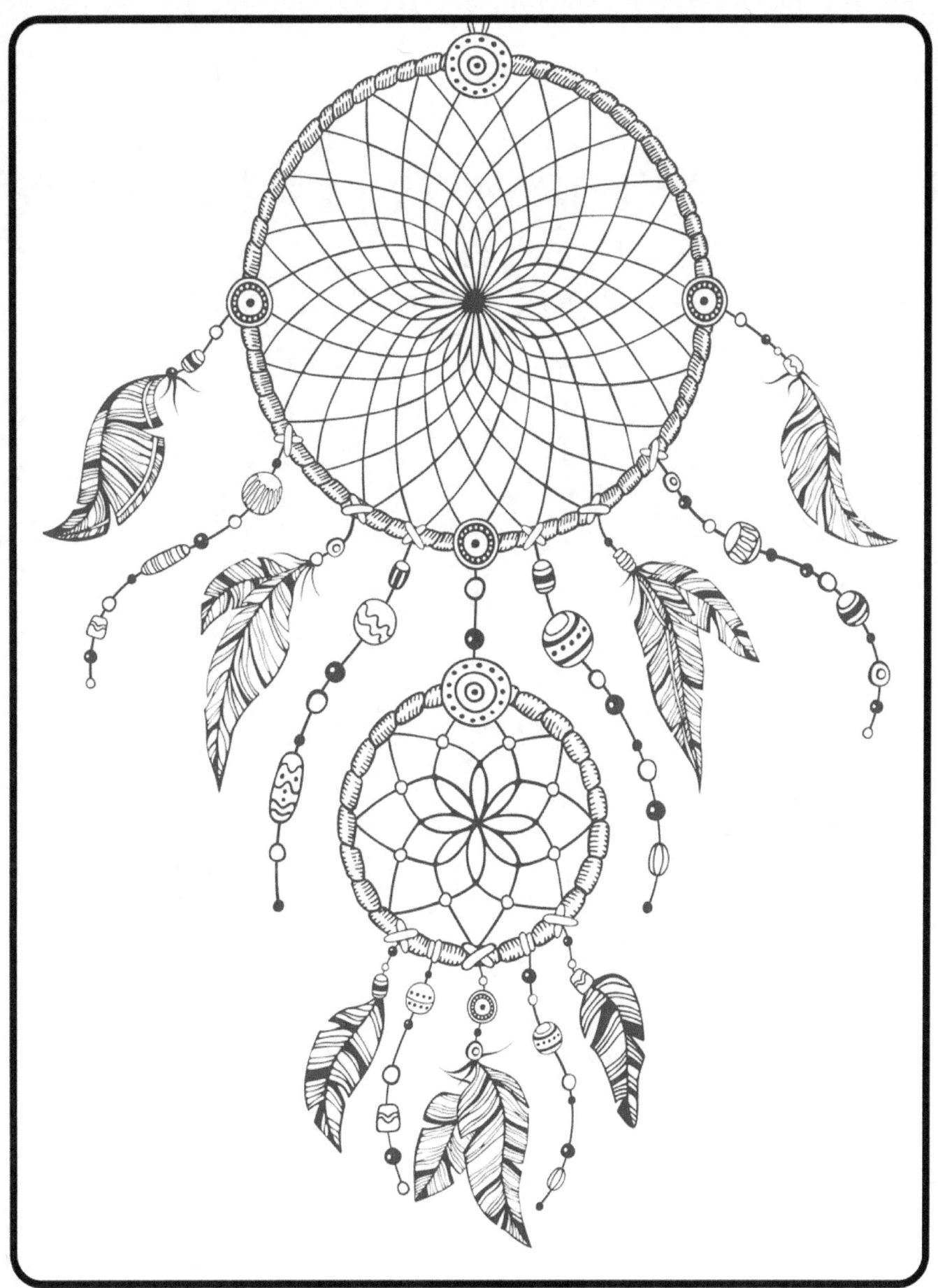

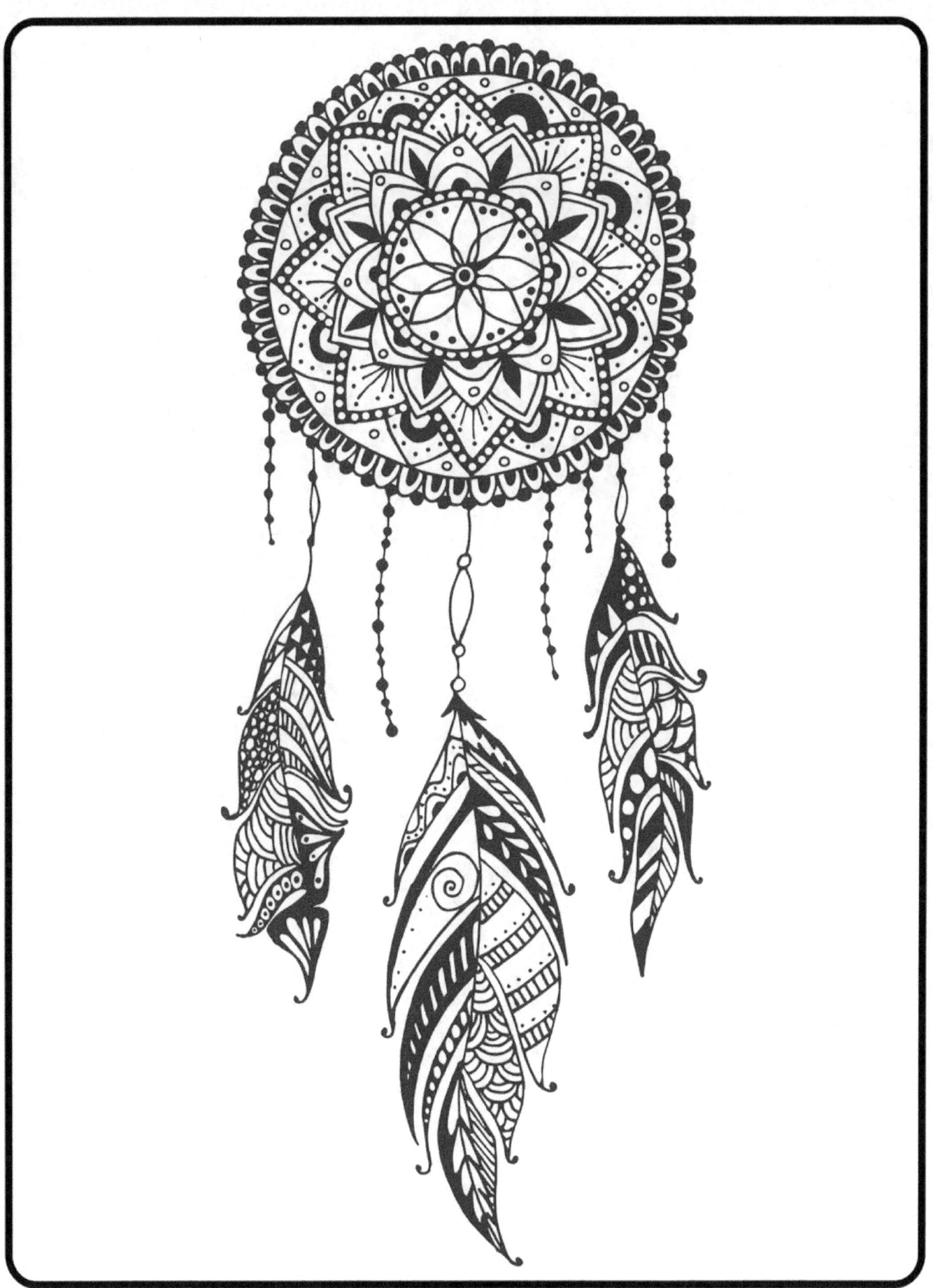

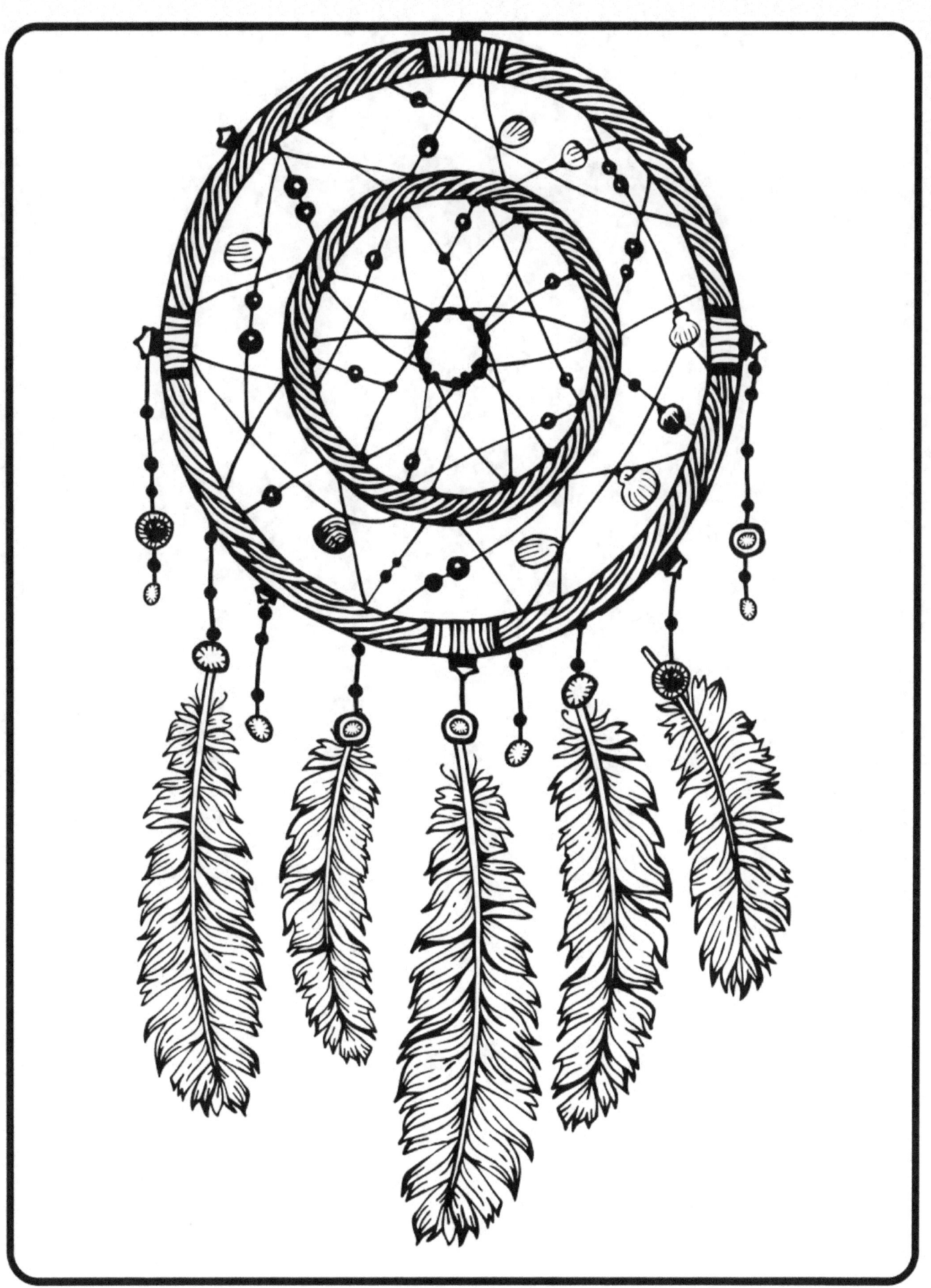

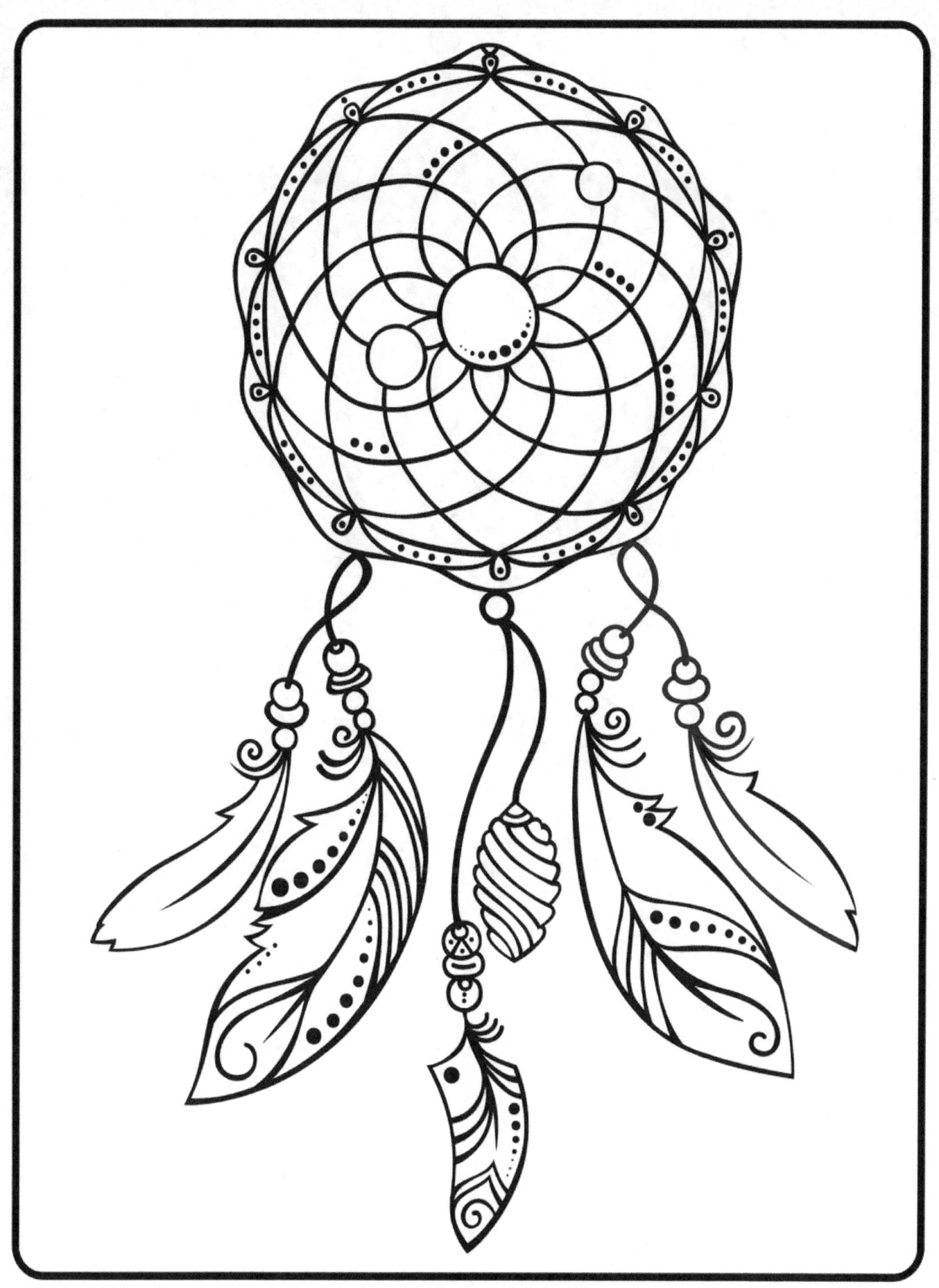

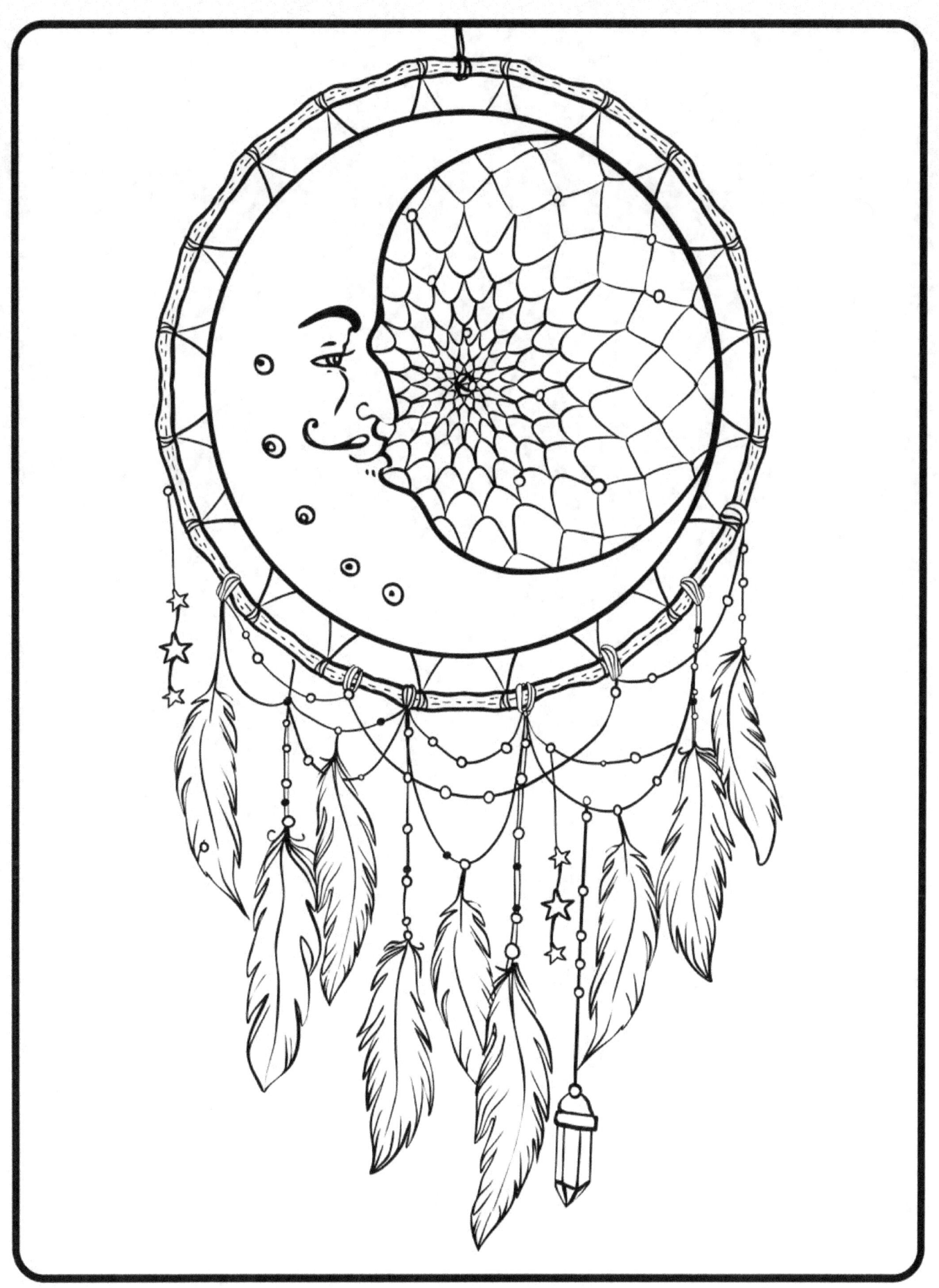

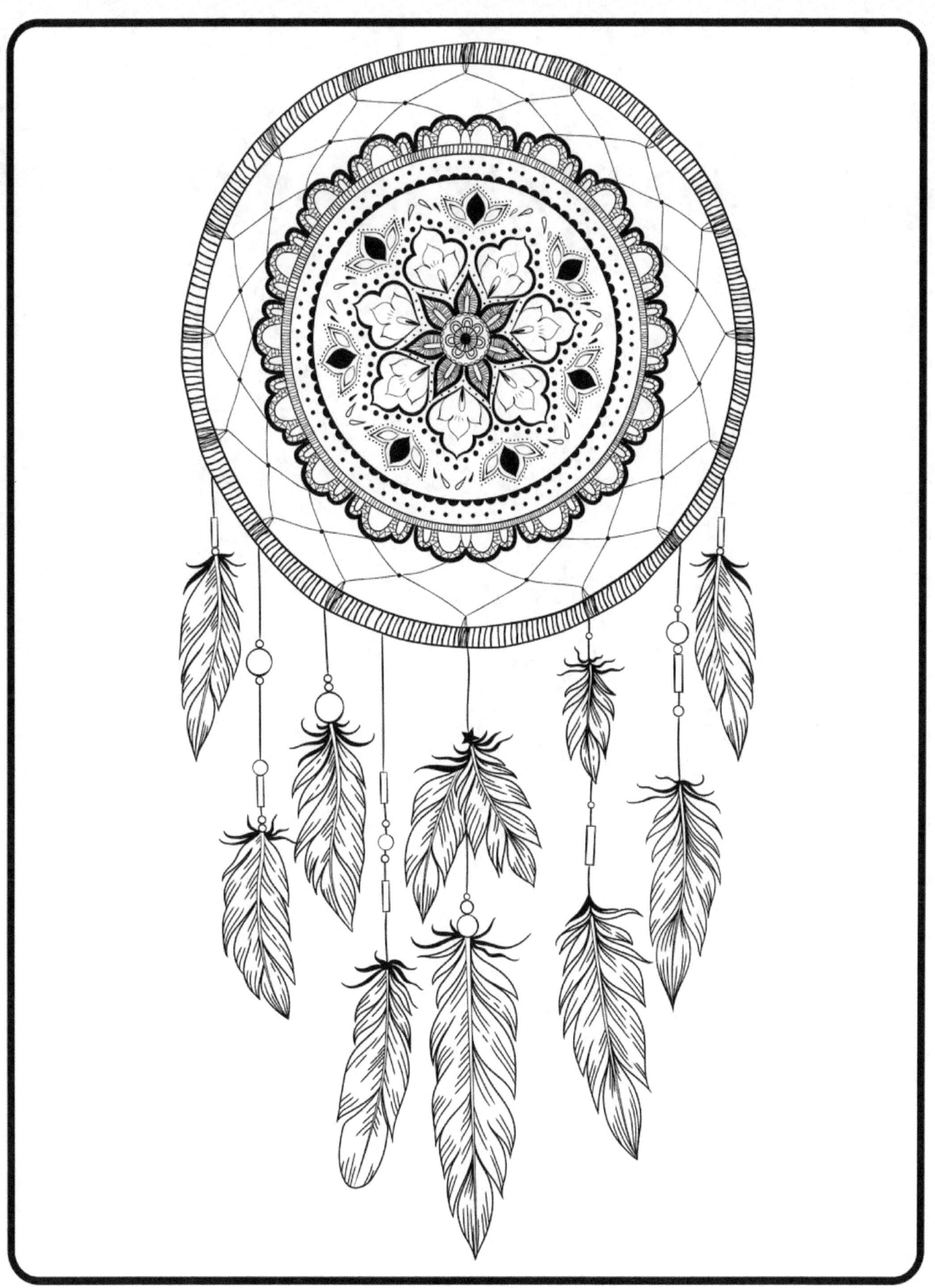

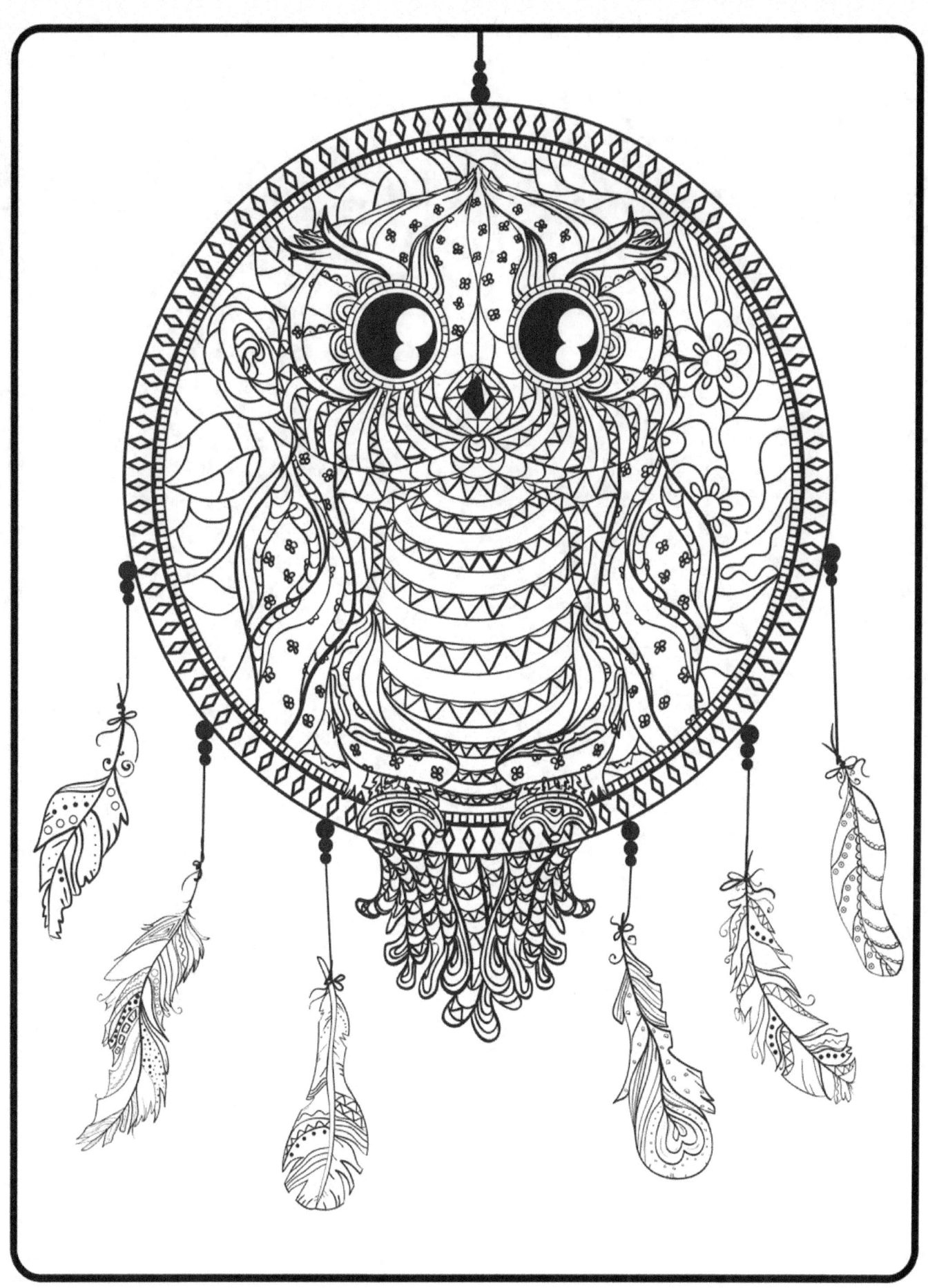

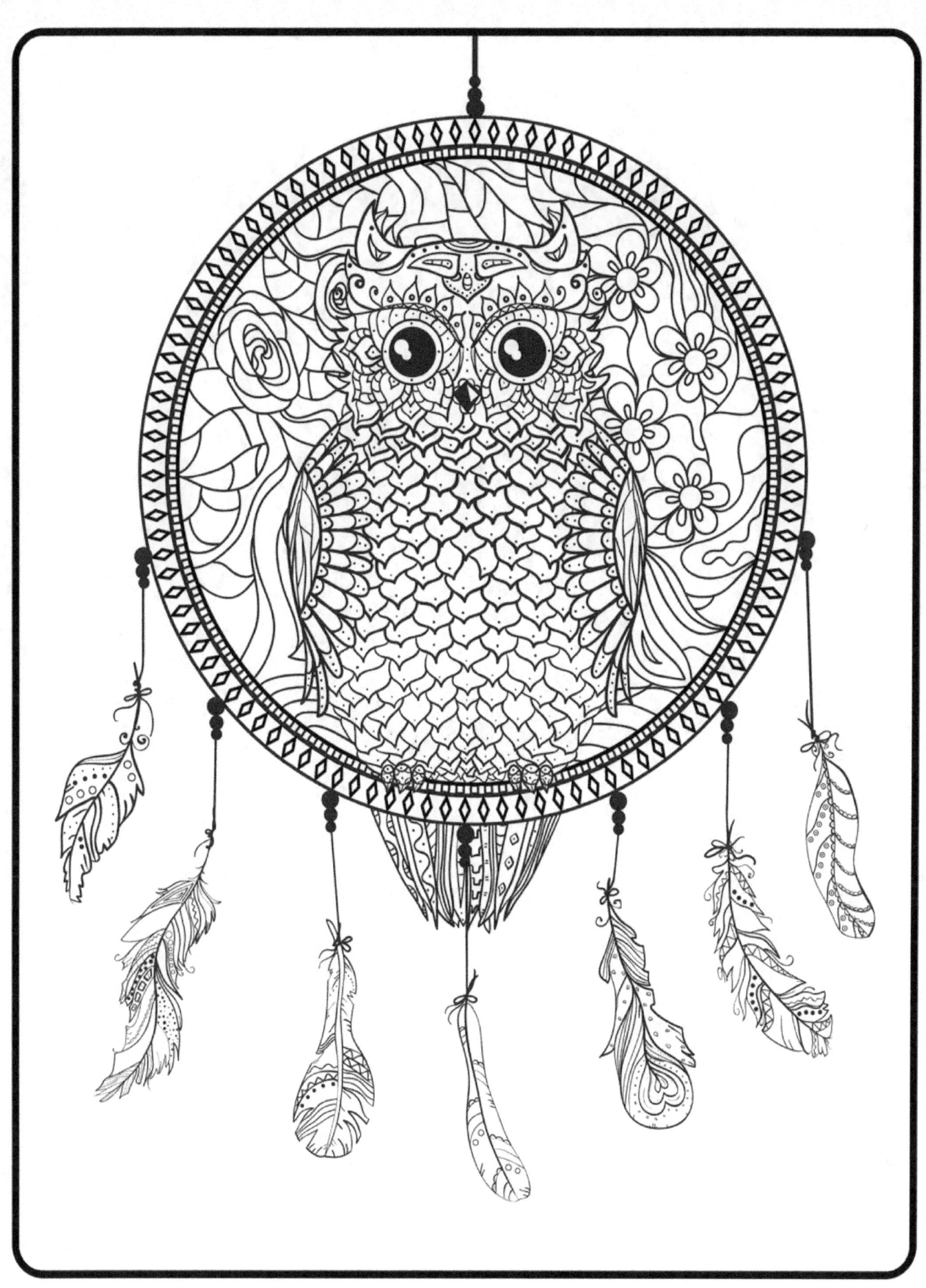

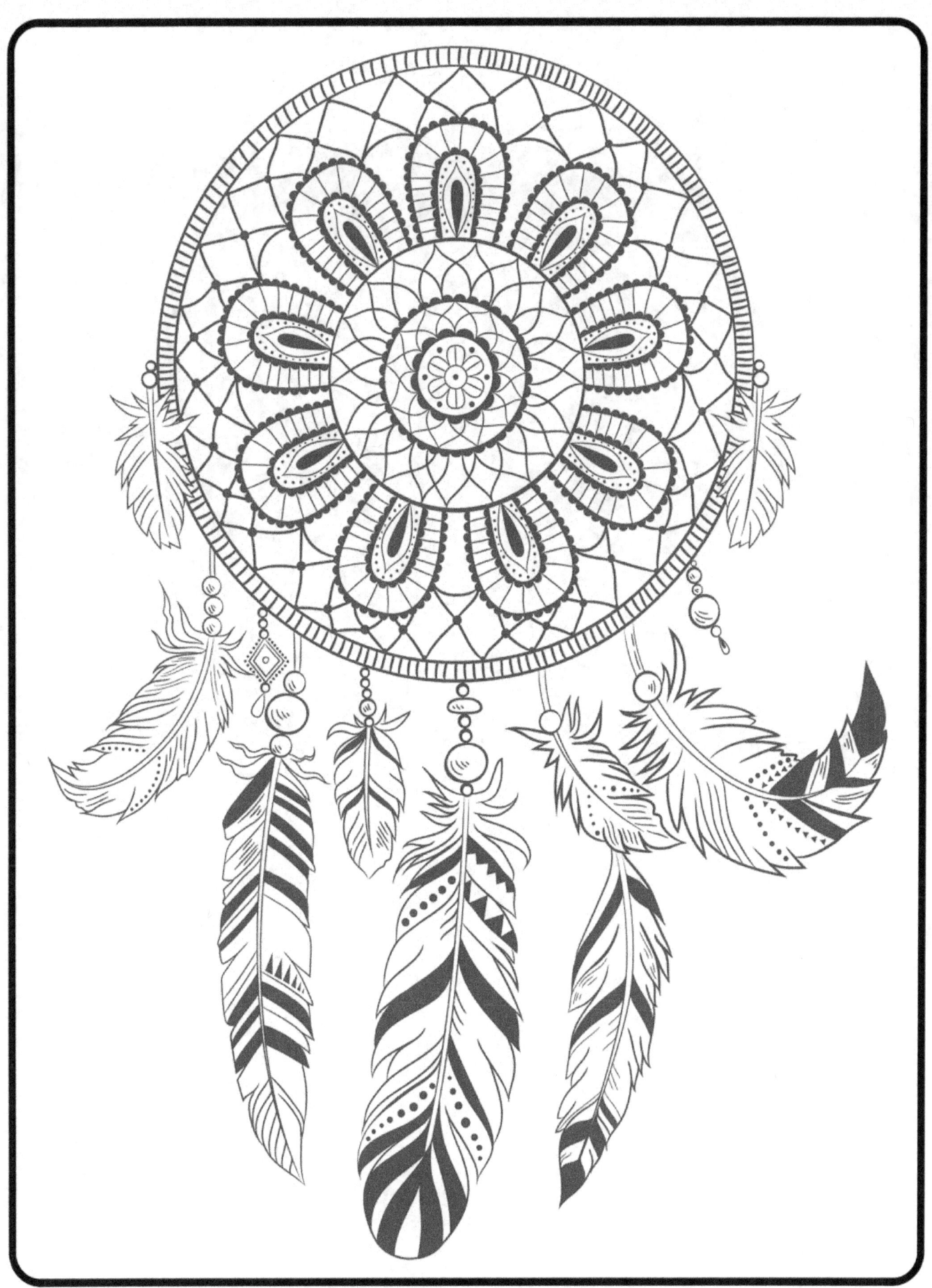

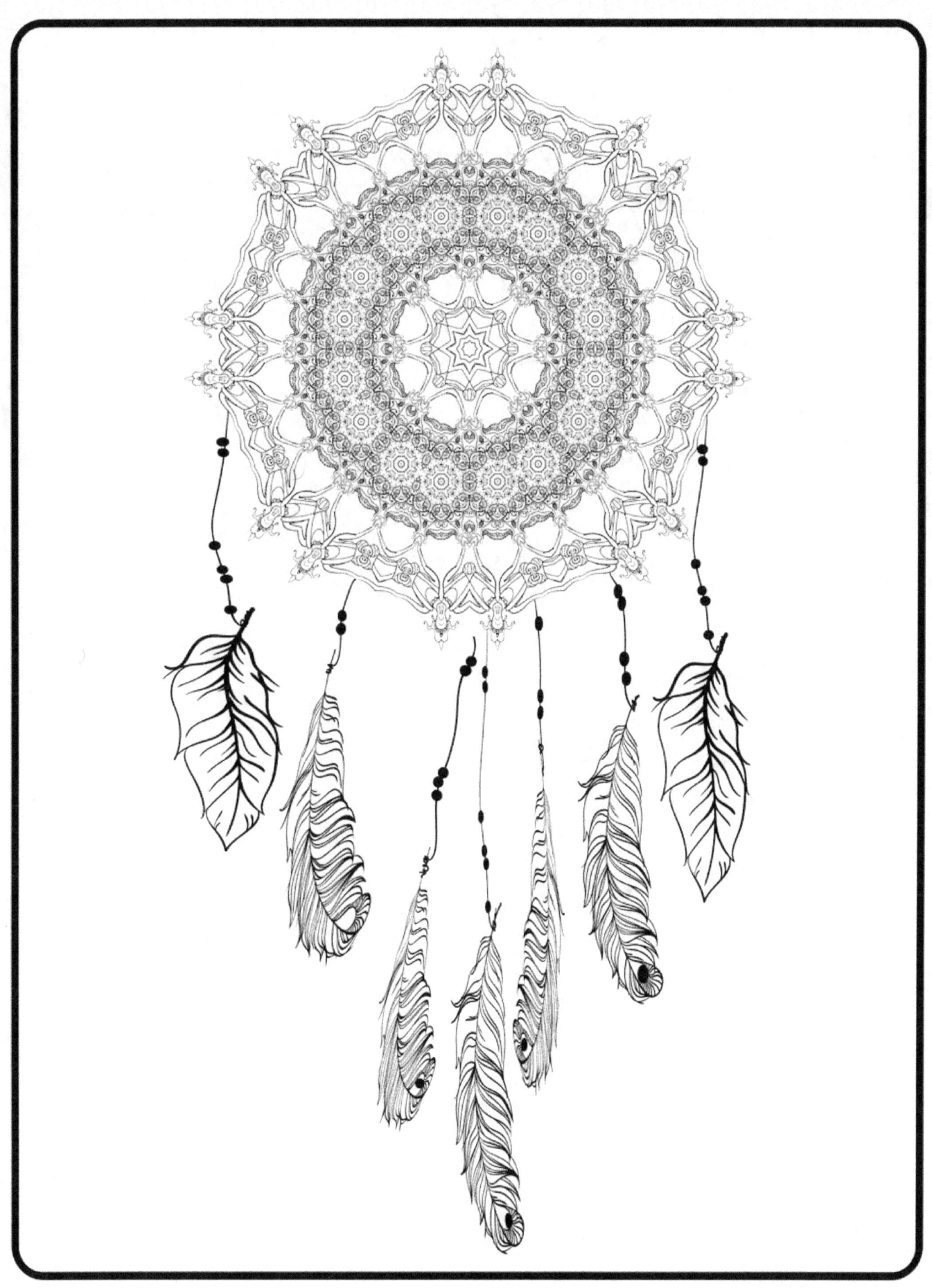

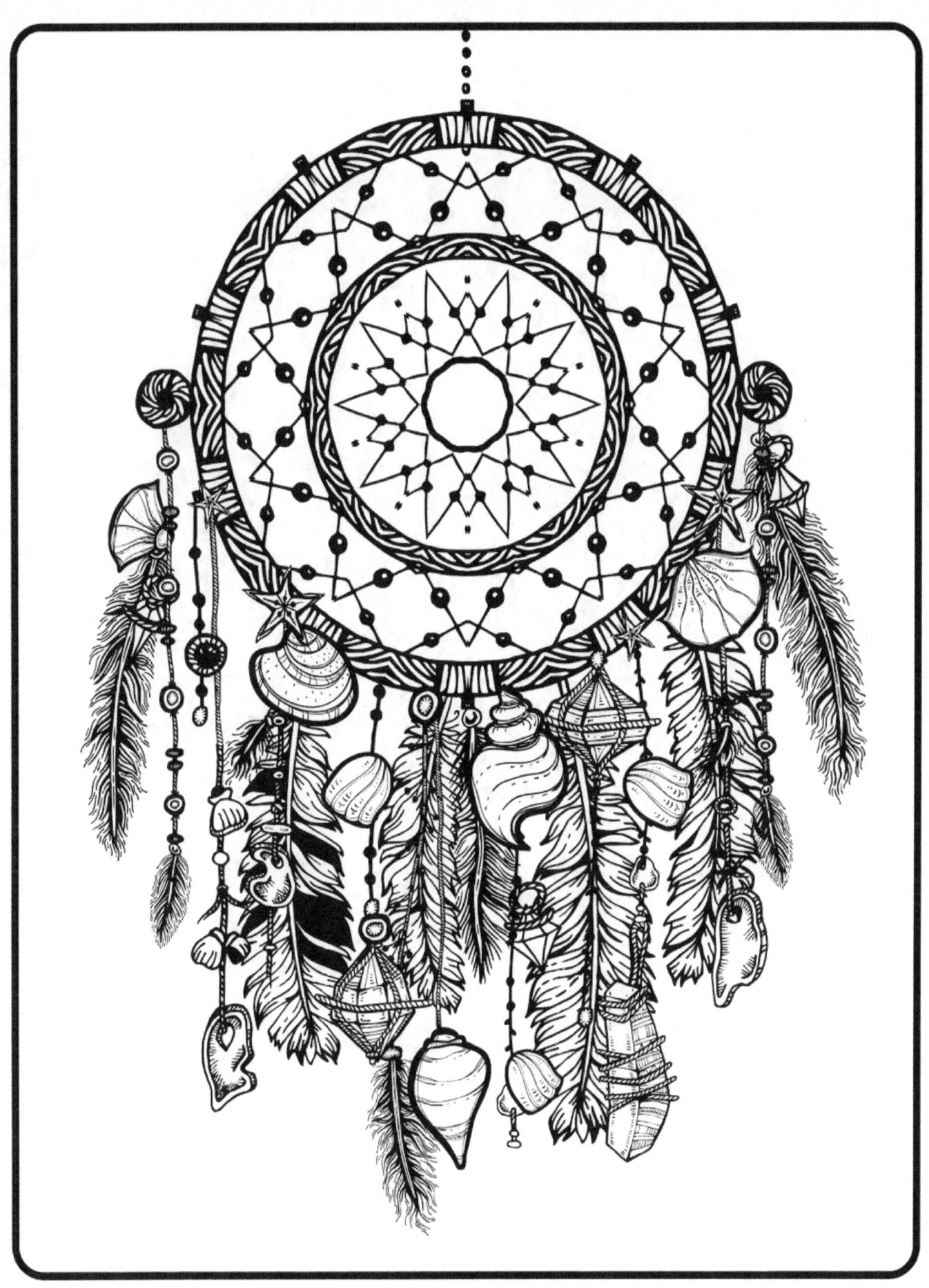

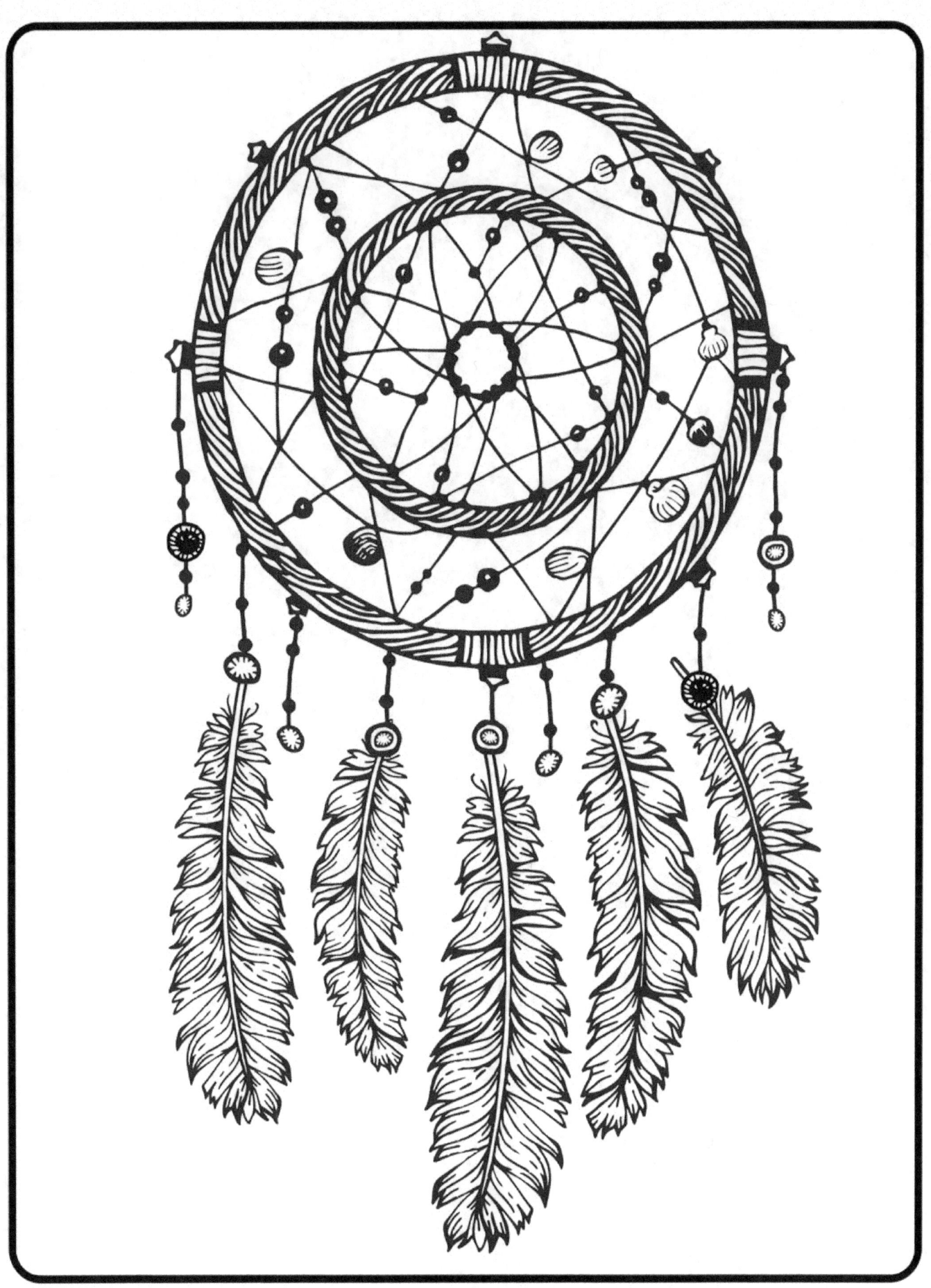

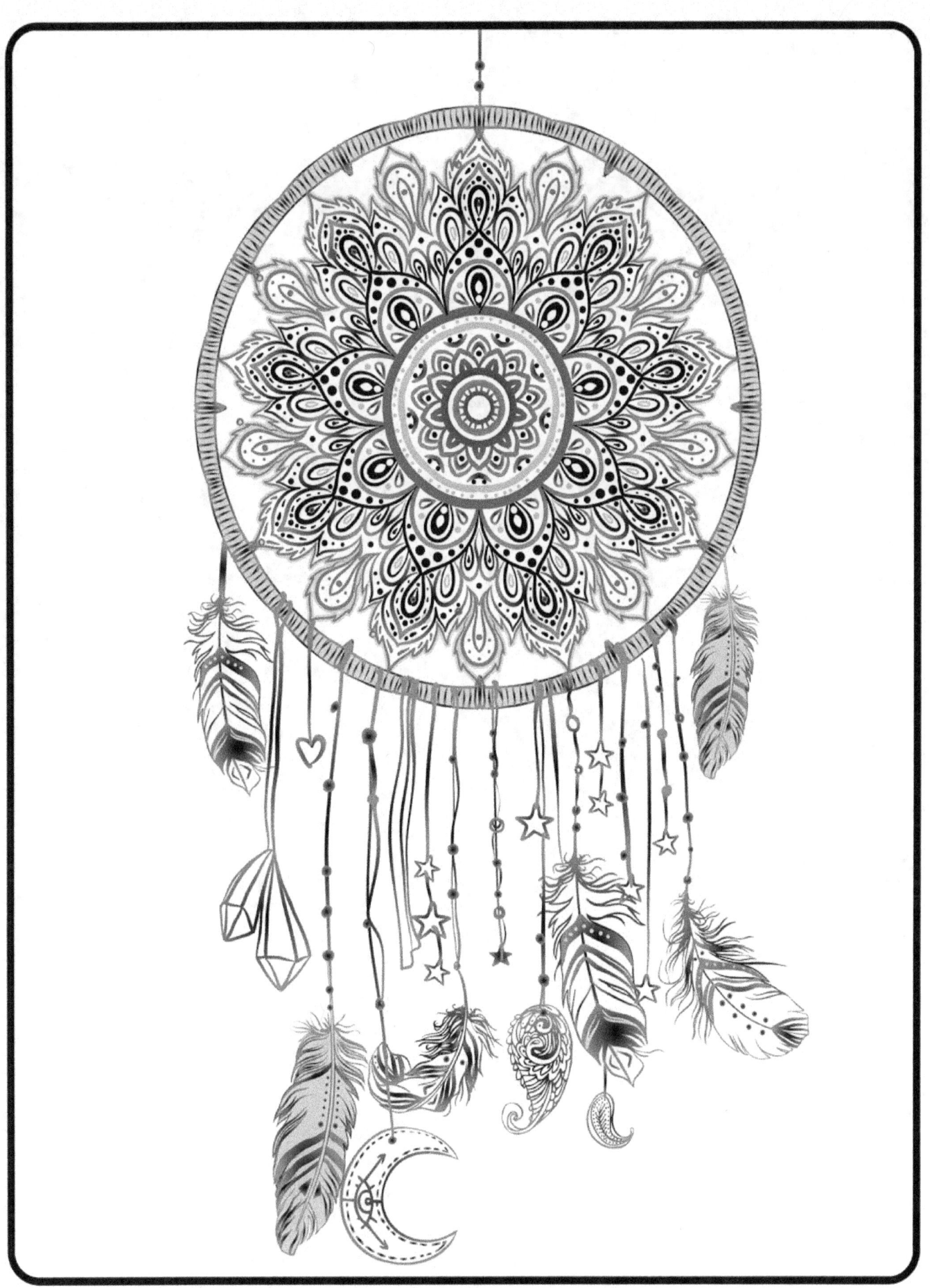

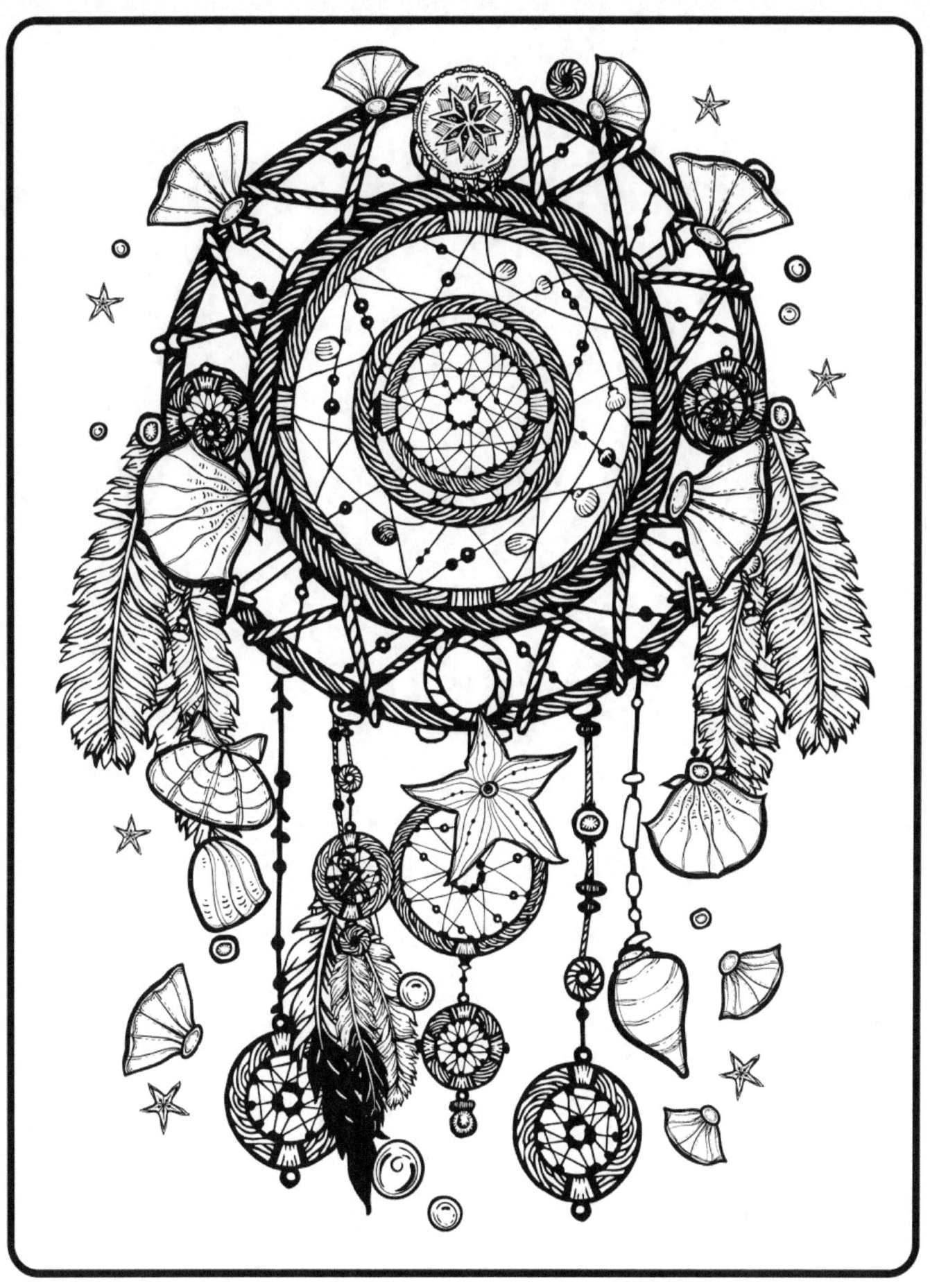

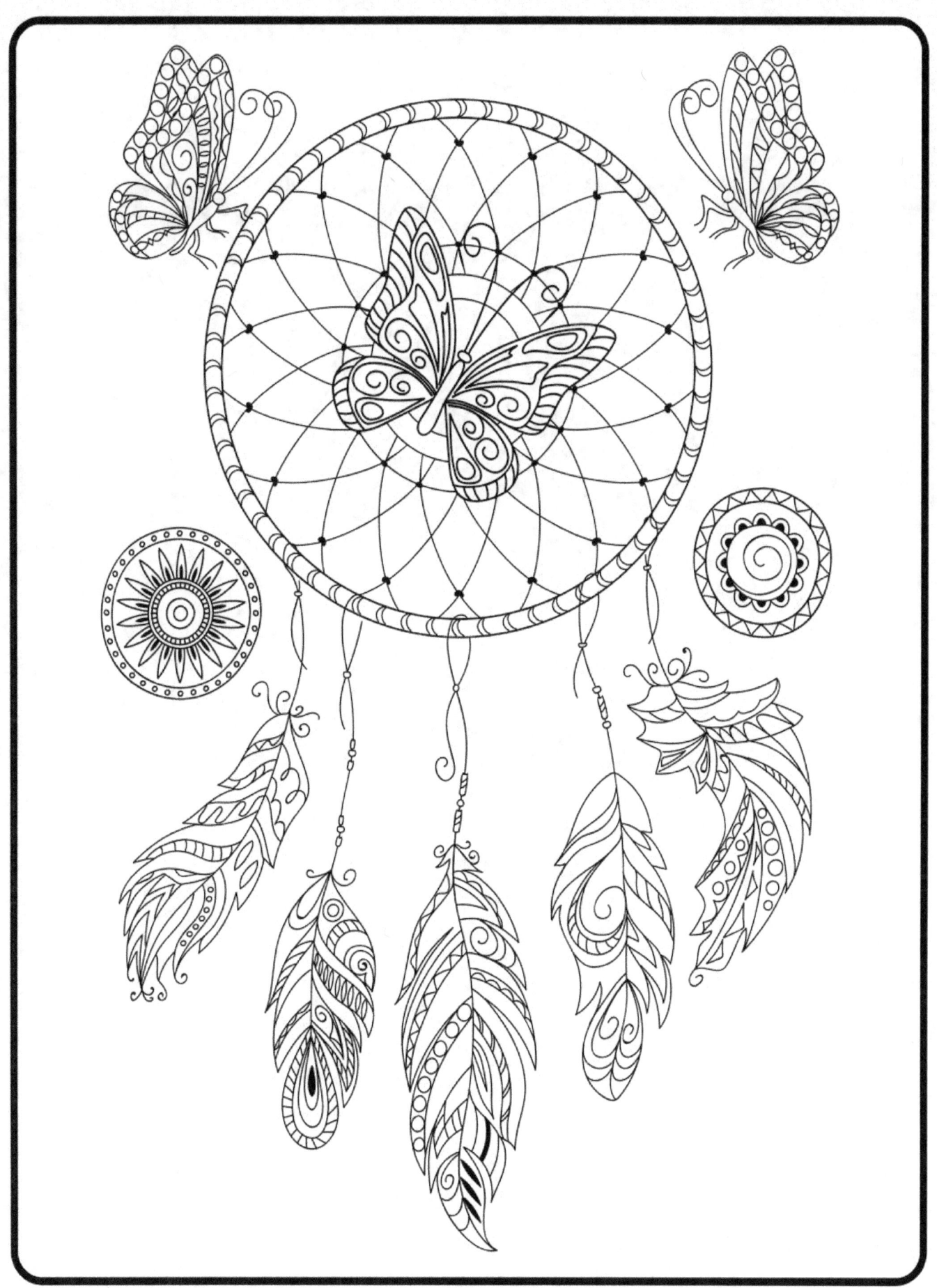

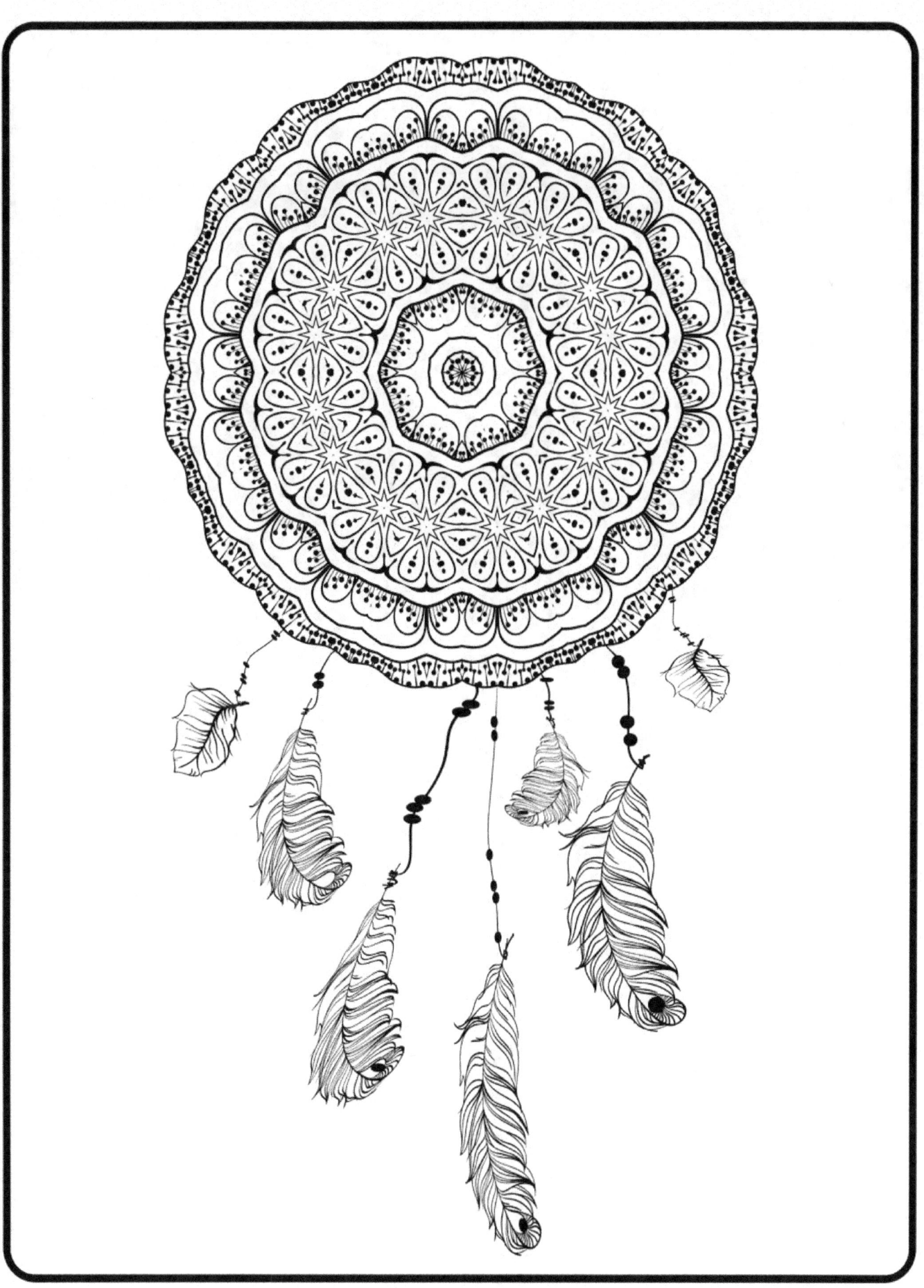

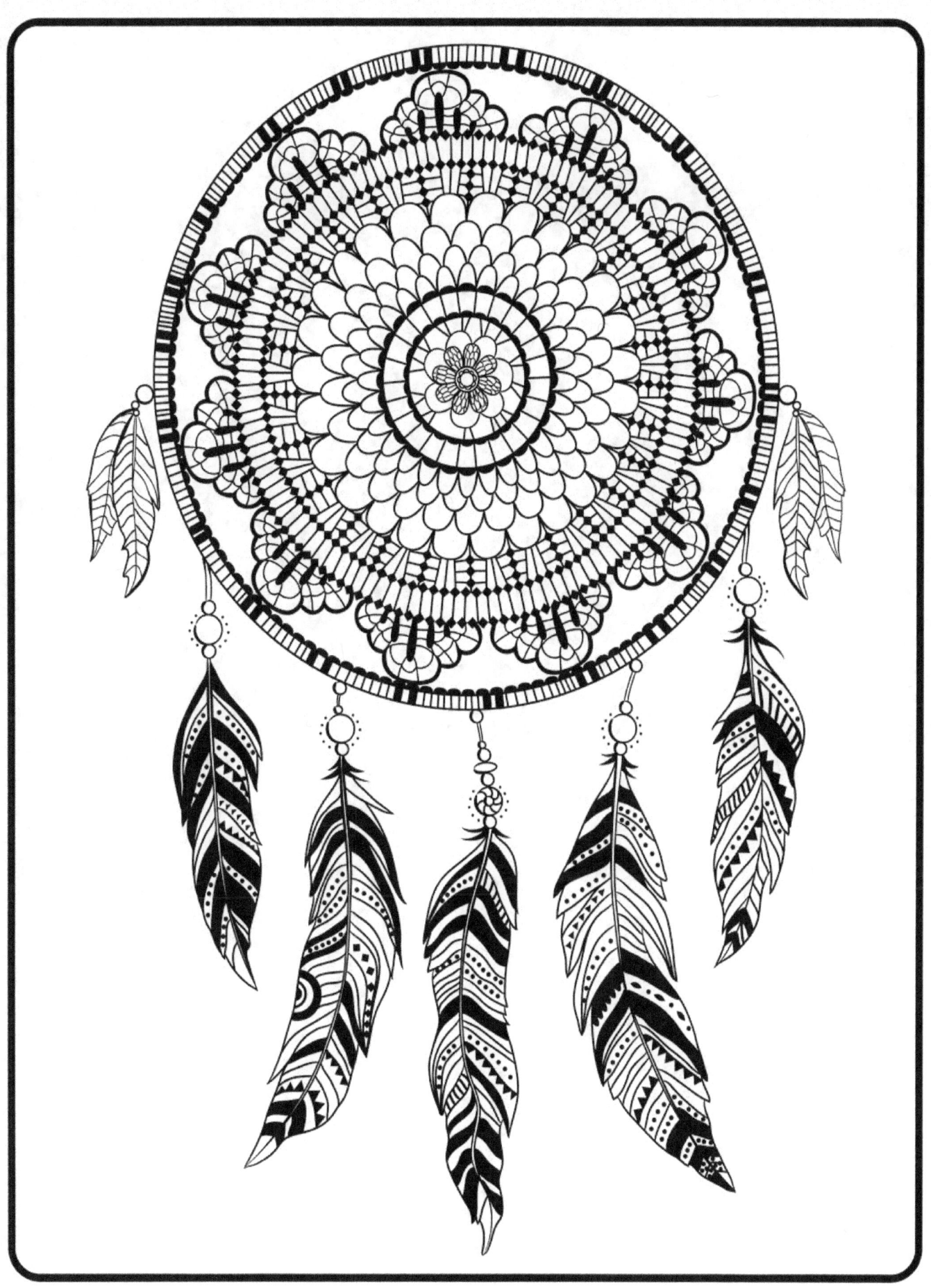

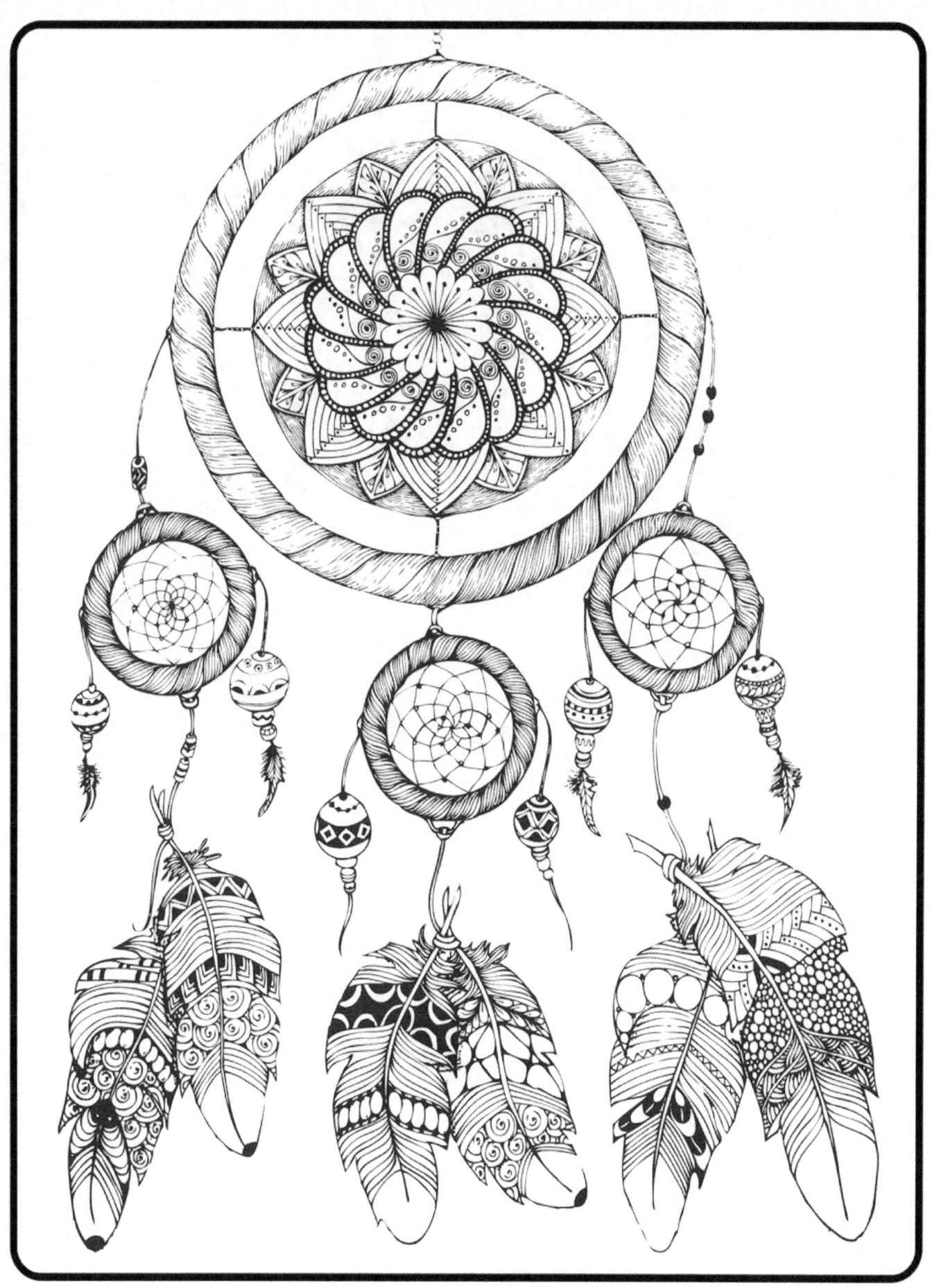

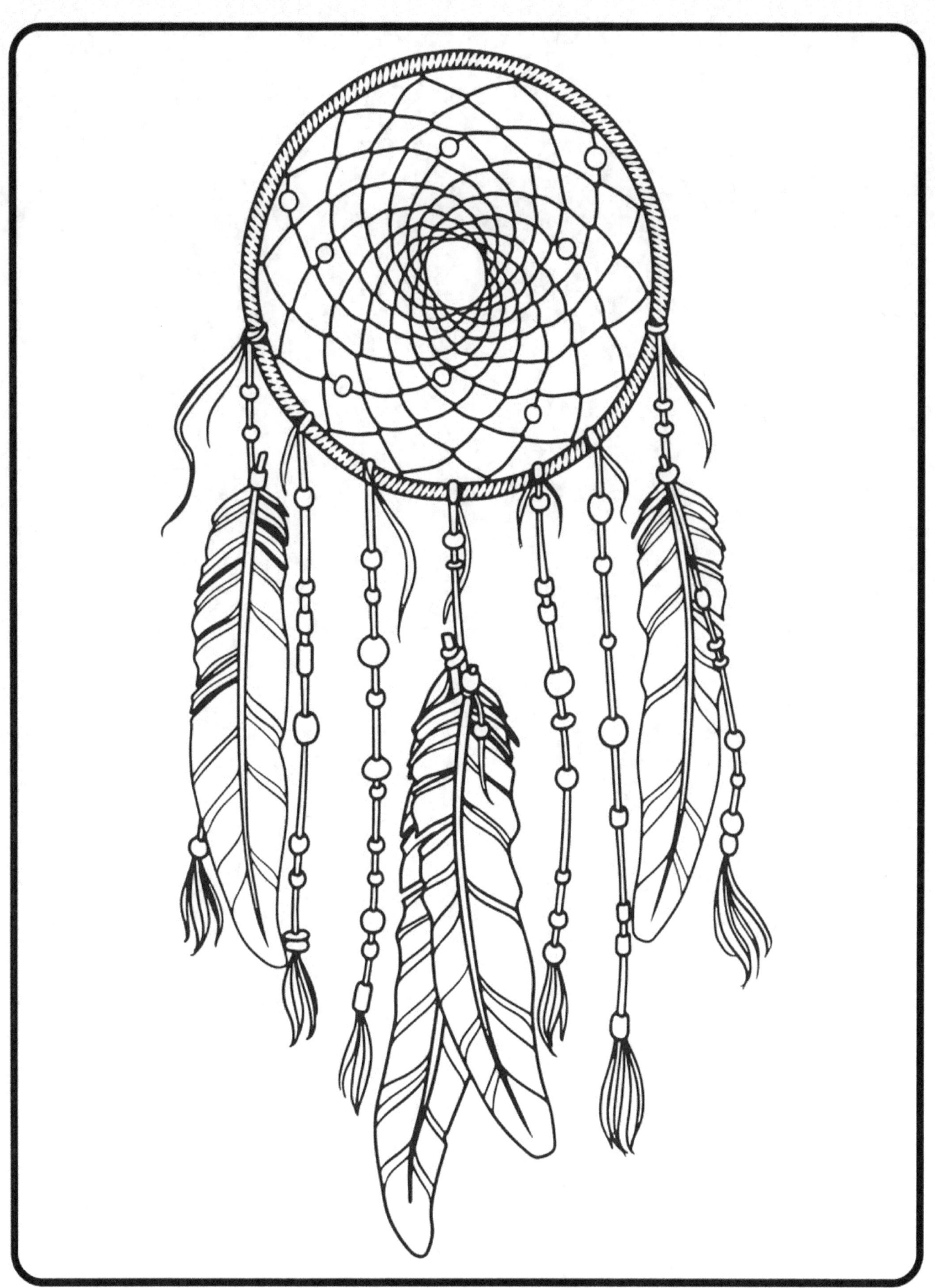

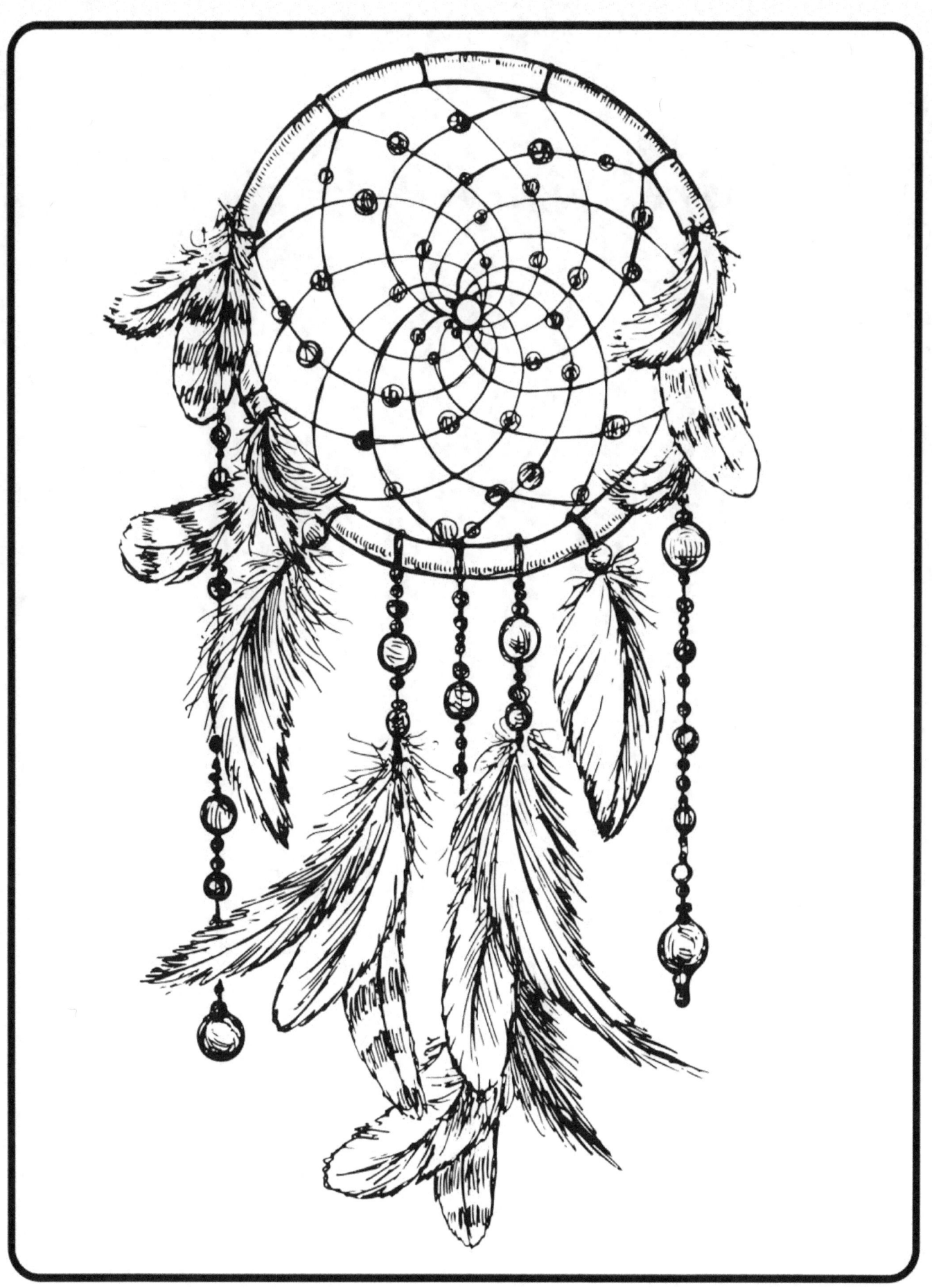

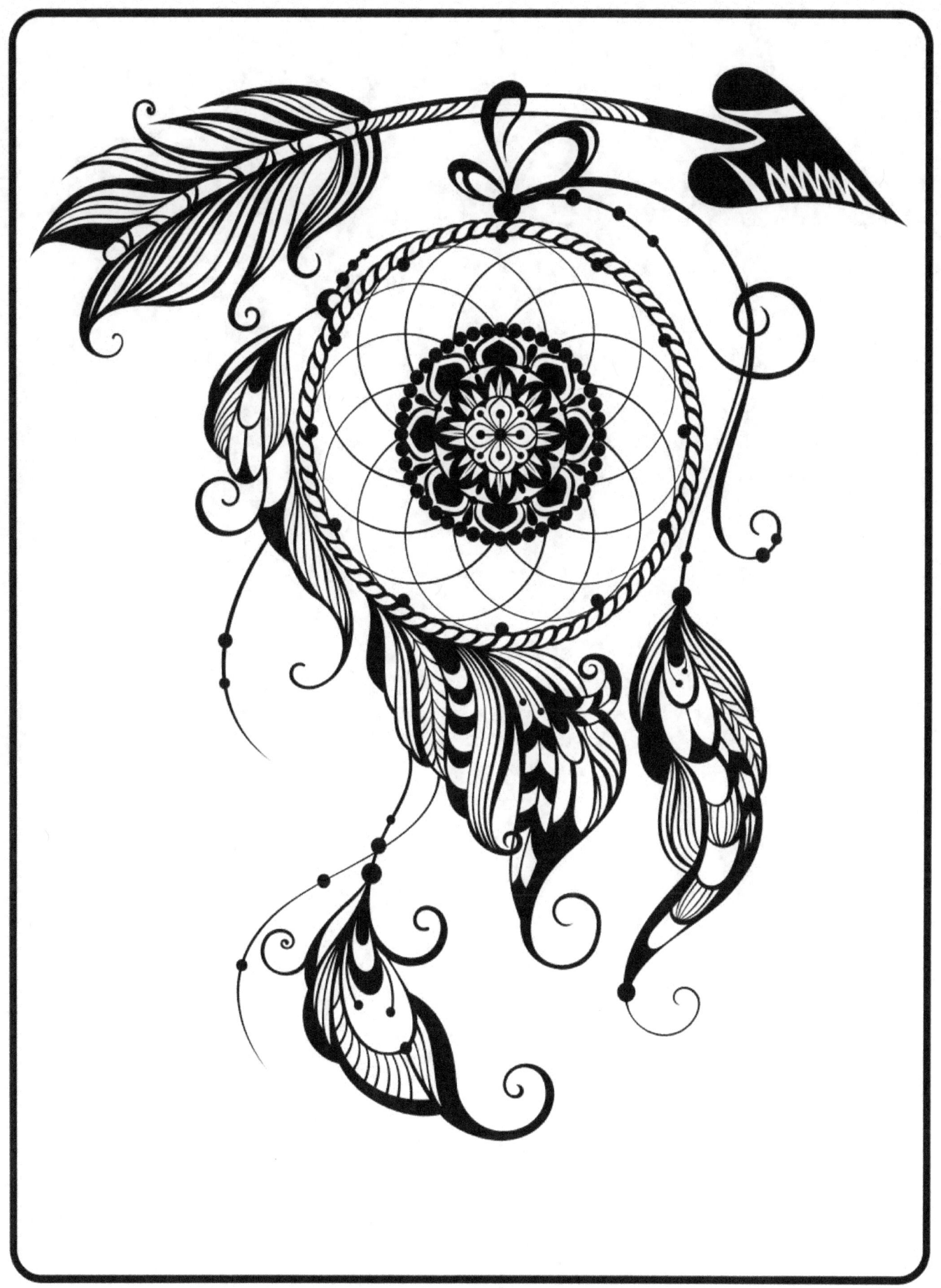

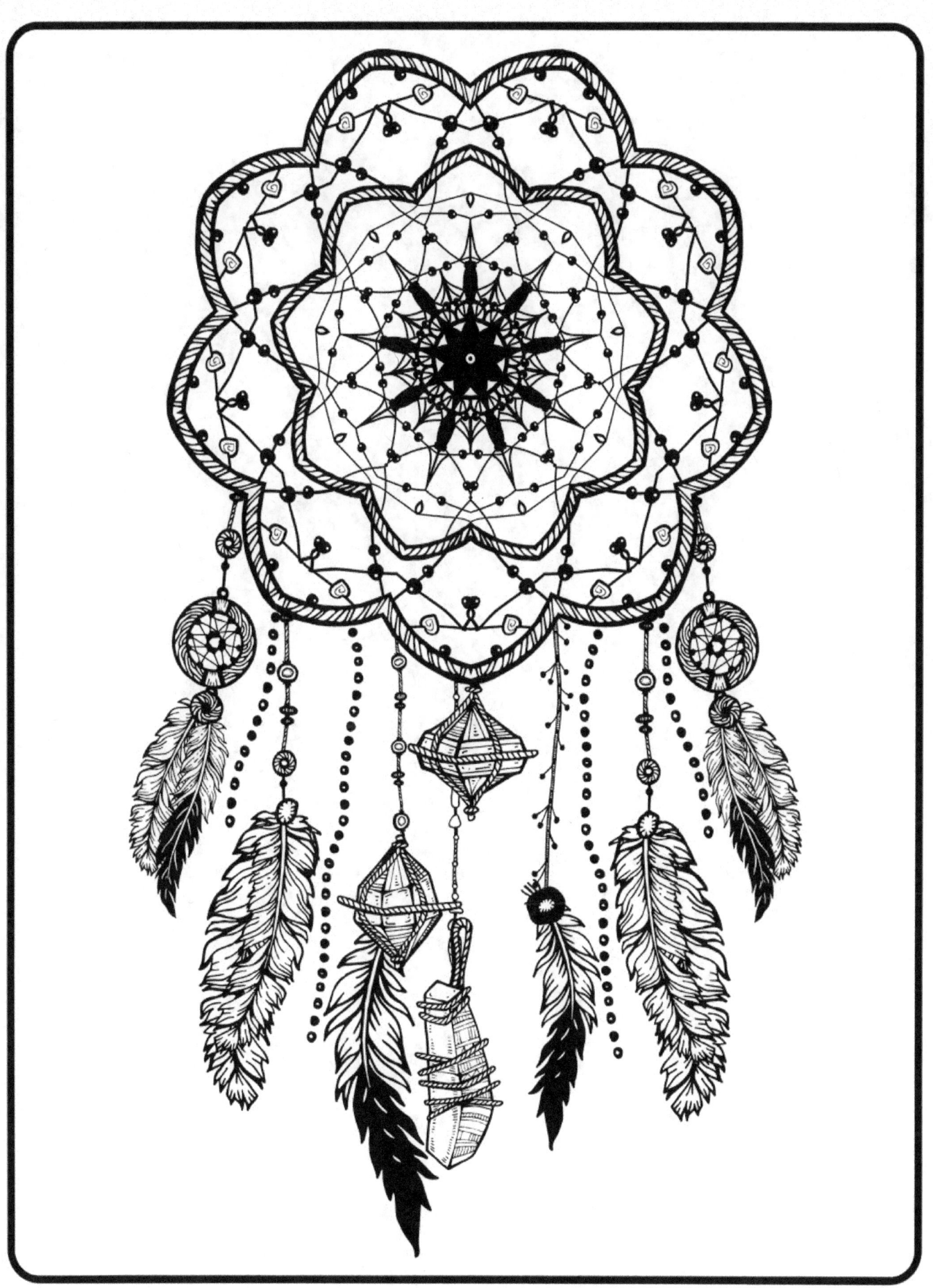

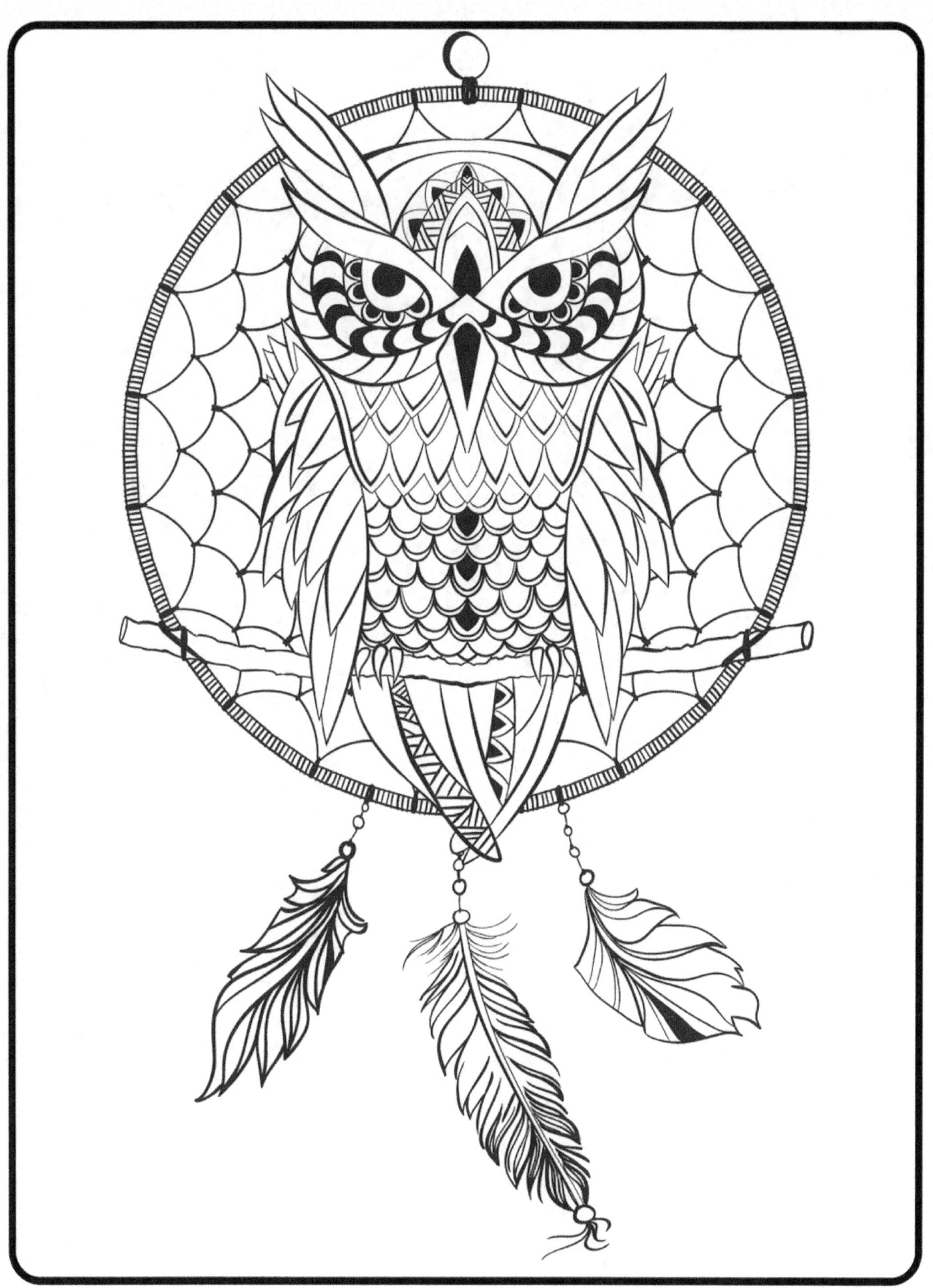

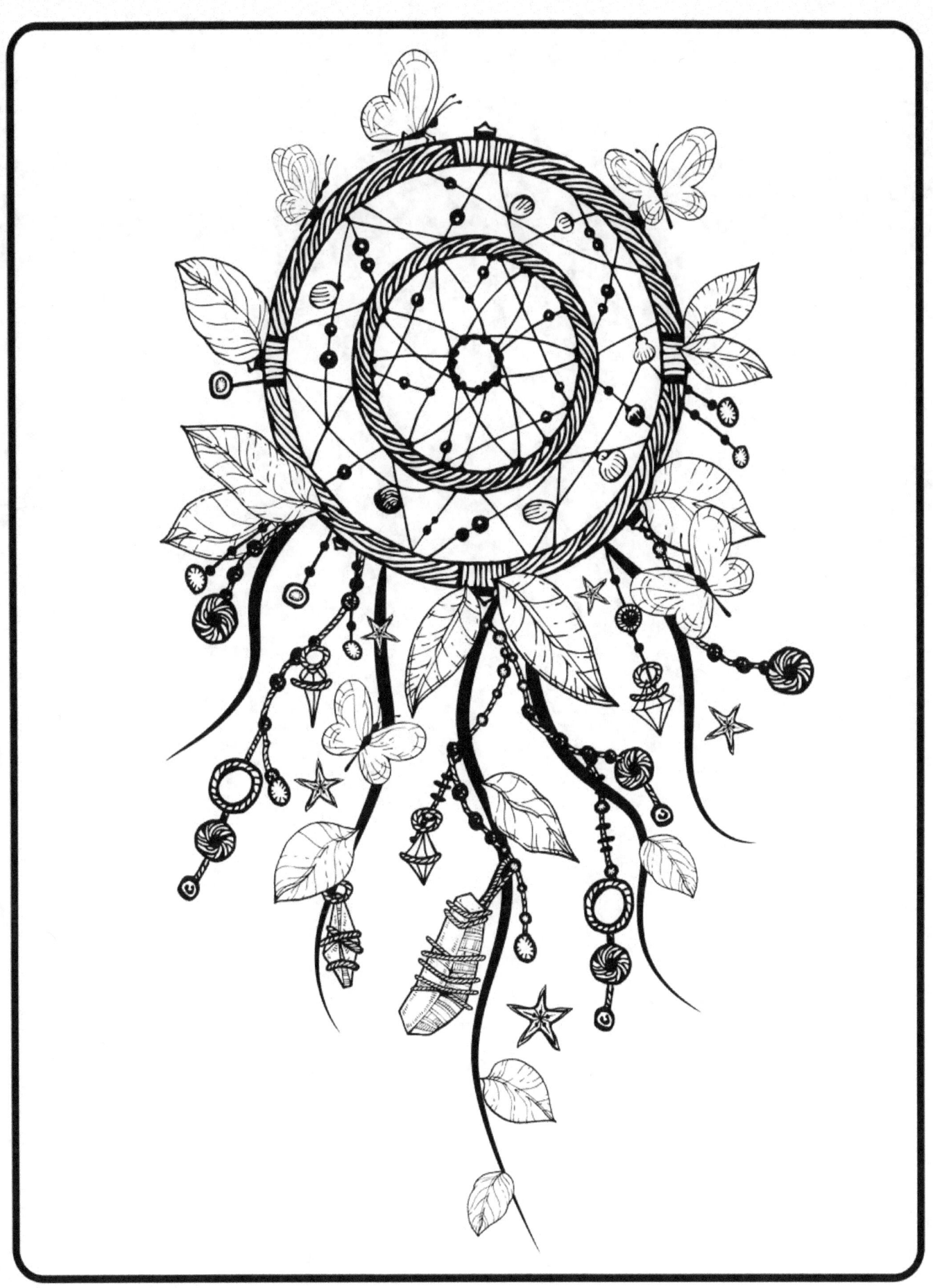

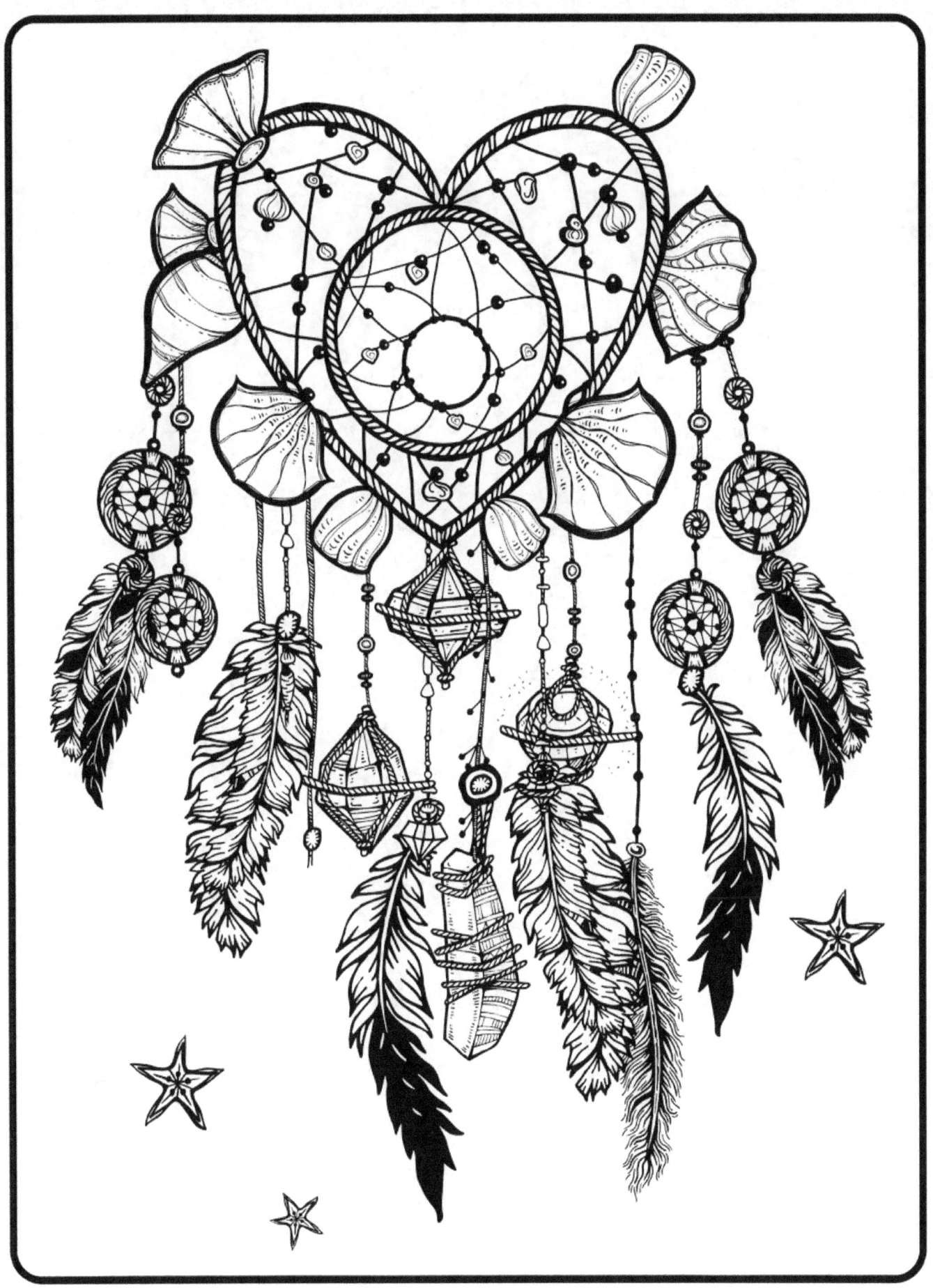

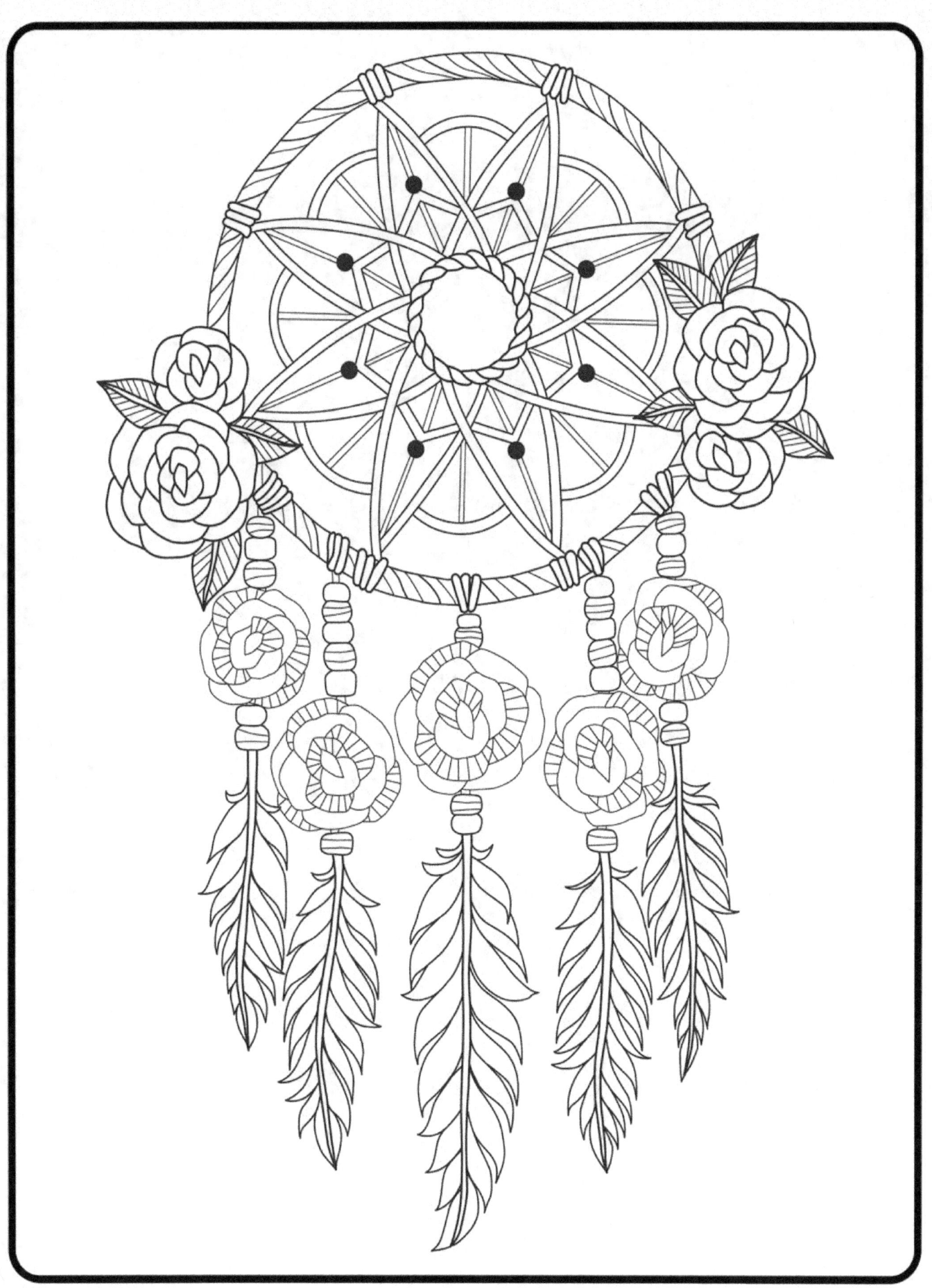

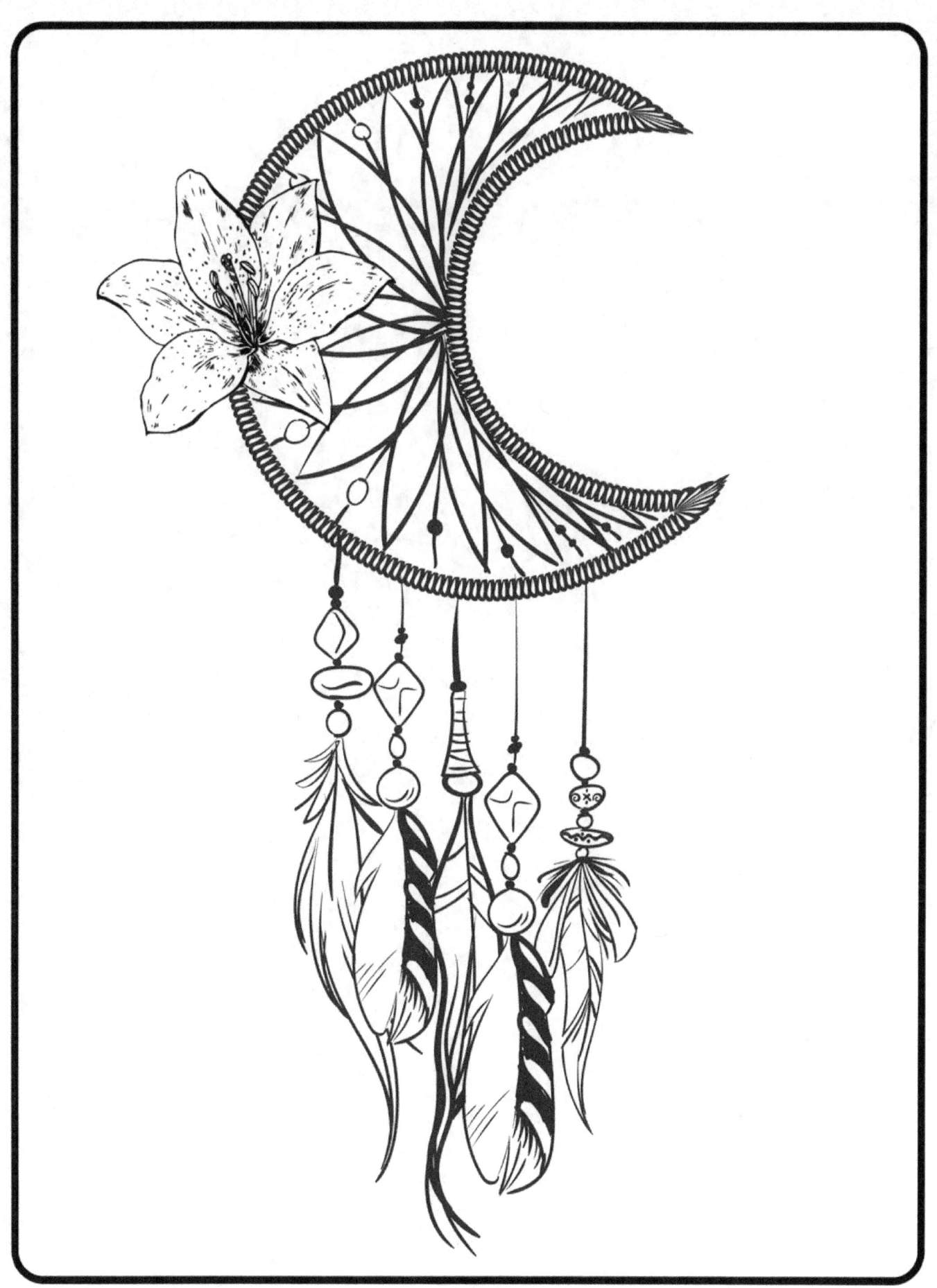

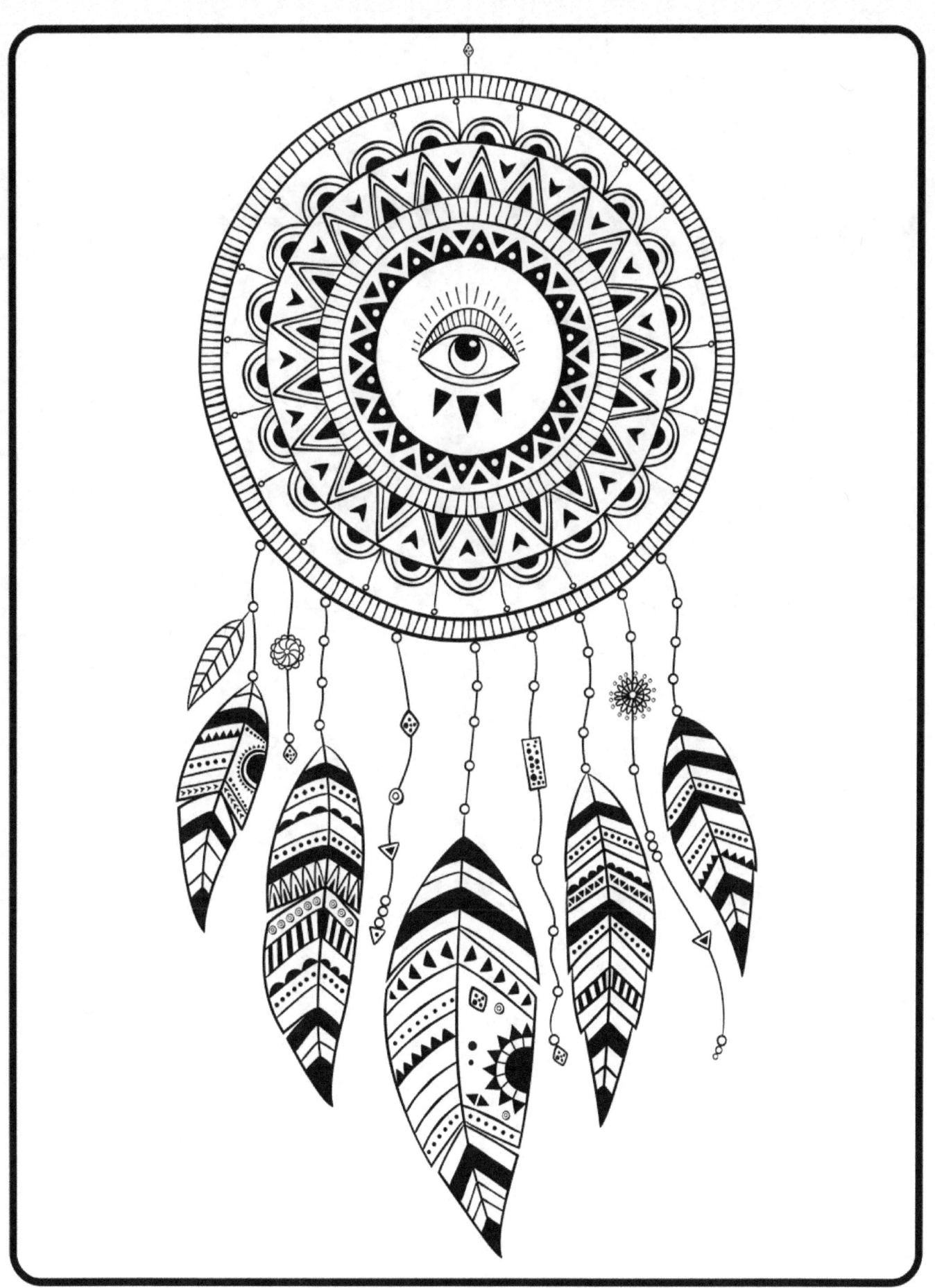

# More coloring books from Katrin Stark

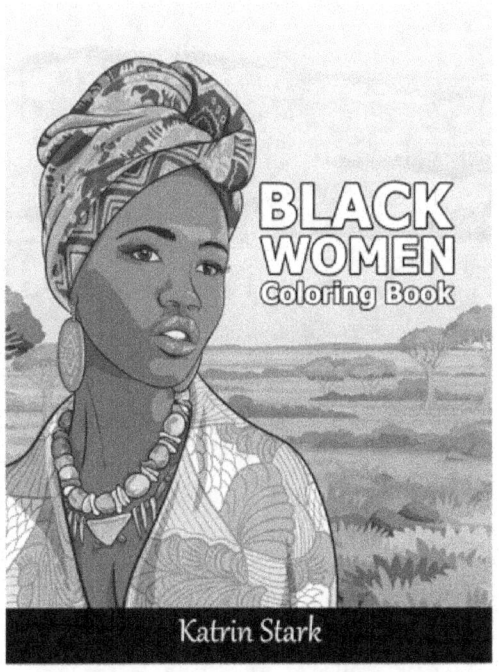

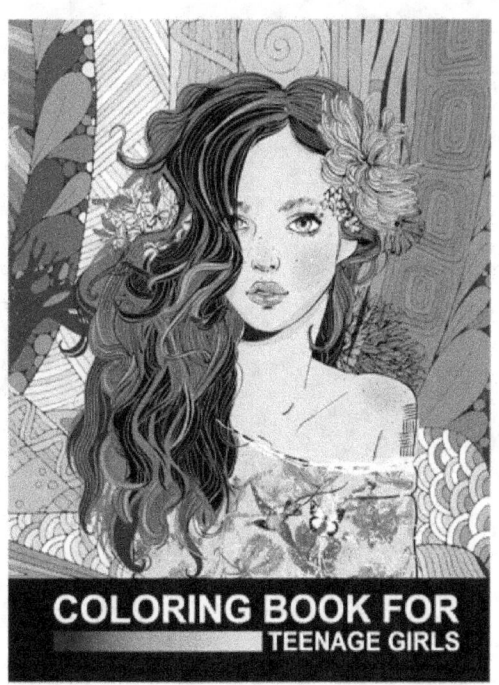

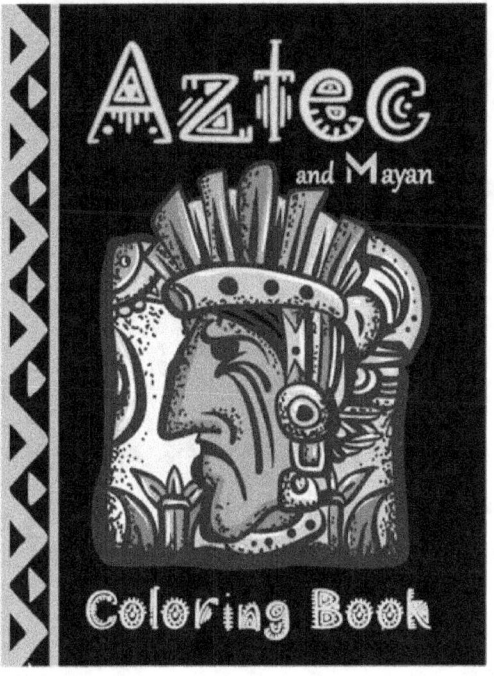

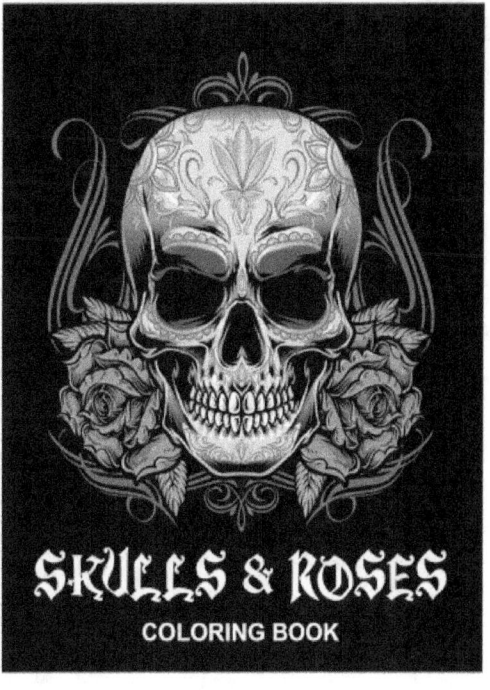

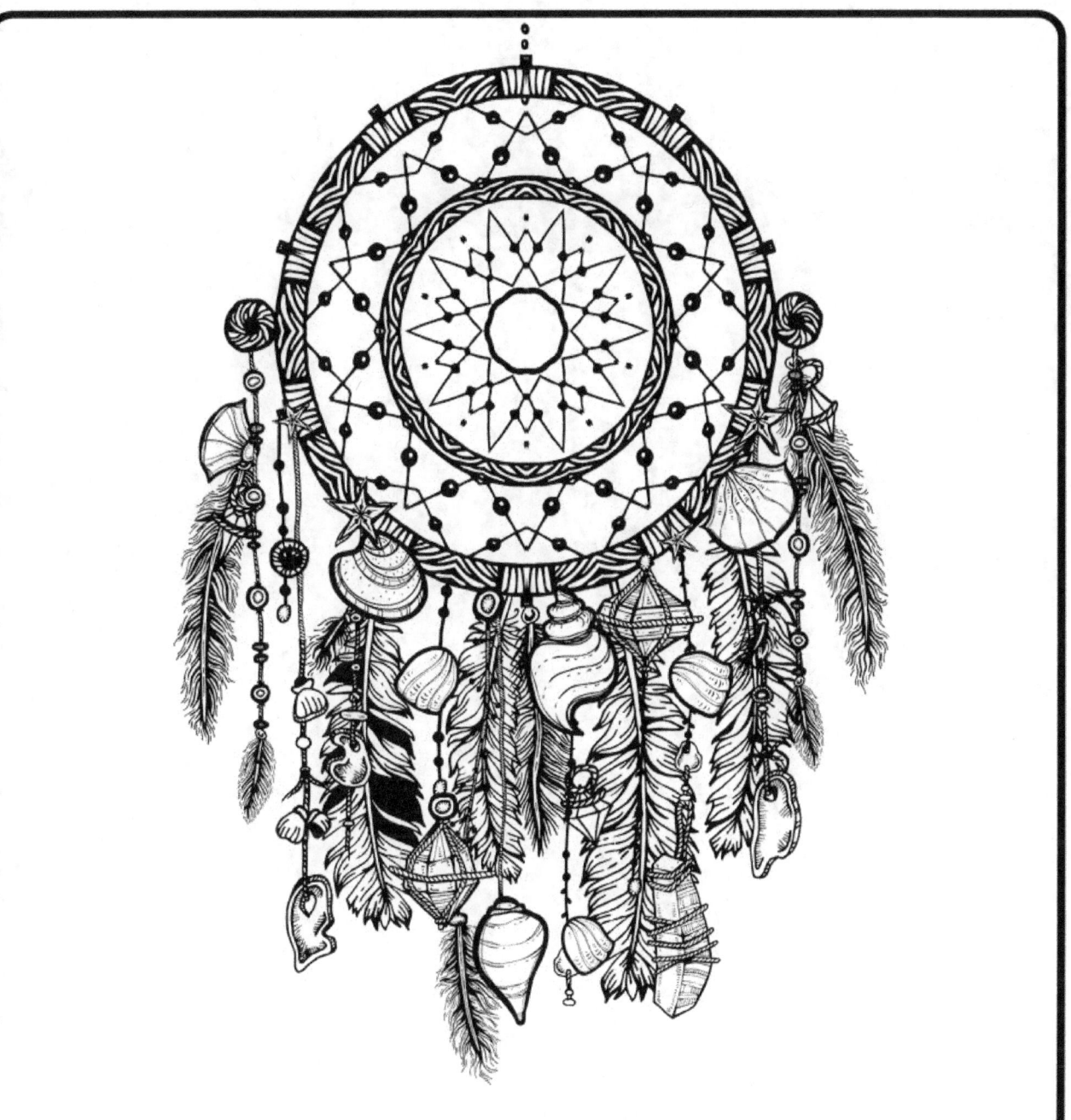

# Thank you for buying this book

If you like the book, please consider leaving a review,

it will help author to create better books in the future

www.amazon.com/Katrin-Stark
www.amazon.co.uk/Katrin-Stark

www.ingramcontent.com/pod-product-compliance
Lightning Source LLC
Chambersburg PA
CBHW080859220526
45467CB00008B/2570